THE GOSPEL OF JESUS

THE GOSPEL OF JESUS

A TRUE STORY

BEN WITHERINGTON III

 seedbed

Scripture taken from the Common English Bible®, CEB® Copyright © 2010, 2011 by Common English Bible.™ Used by permission. All rights reserved worldwide.

"Christus Paradox" by Sylvia Dunstan Copyright © 1991 by GIA Publications, Inc. 7404 S. Mason Ave., Chicago, IL 60638, www.giamusic.com 800.442.1358. All rights reserved. Used by permission.

Printed in the United States of America

Paperback ISBN: 978-1-62824-071-9
Mobi ISBN: 978-1-62824-072-6
ePub ISBN: 978-1-62824-073-3
uPDF ISBN: 978-1-62824-074-0

Library of Congress Control Number: 2014931391

Cover illustration by Henryk Siemiradzki, Christ in the House of Martha and Mary
Cover design by Sarah Immerfall
Page design by PerfecType, Nashville, Tennessee

SEEDBED PUBLISHING
Franklin, Tennessee
seedbed.com
Sowing for a Great Awakening

This book is dedicated to my Nashville friend, A. J.,
who probably understands "the most misunderstood Jew"
better than I do.
Someday I hope to see him fully with your eyes,
or maybe we will get to do that together in the Kingdom.
I hope so.

Incognito

He came incognito,
A thinly veiled disguise.
The not-so-subtle Son of Man,
A human with God's eyes.

The messianic secret
Left many unawares
That God had walked upon the earth
And shared our human cares.

We did not see his glory,
At least not at first glimpse.
It took an Easter wake-up call,
Before it all made sense.

The truth of Incarnation,
Of dwelling within flesh,
Shows goodness in creation,
And Word of God made fresh.

Standing on the boundary
Twixt earth and heaven above,
A Jew who hailed from Nazareth,
But came from God's great love.

Born of humble parents,
Laid down inside a stall,
This king required no entourage,
No pomp or folderol.

No person was beneath him,
No angel o'er his head.
He came to serve the human race,
To raise it from the dead.

His death a great conundrum:
How can the Deathless die?
But if he had not bowed his head,
Life would have passed us by.

Though we are dying to be loved,
And long for endless life,
He was dying in his love,
And thereby ending strife.

Perhaps the incognito
Belongs instead to us,
Who play at being human,
And fail to be gold dust.

But there was once a God-man
Who played the human's part,
And lived and died and rose again,
Made sin and death depart.

Yet now through a glass dimly,
We see the visage royal,
And feebly honor his great worth
And his atoning toil.

We cannot see his Spirit,
But moved by its effects,
We are inspired to praise his worth
And pay our last respects.

Yet, that too brings him glory.
That too makes a start.
The journey of a million miles
Begins within one's heart.

And someday we shall see him
And fully praise his grace;
Someday when heaven and earth collide
And we see face-to-face.

He comes in blinding brilliance,
A not-so-veiled disguise;
The not-so-subtle Son of God,
A God with human eyes.

—Ben Witherington III

Contents

A Note to the Reader

BEFORE THERE WERE four written Gospels, there was the single oral telling of the good news. The world of Jesus was an oral culture. The apostle Paul, for example, uses the phrase "God's word" (singular) in 1 Thessalonians 2:13 to refer to the oral proclamation of this singular story of Jesus that changed their lives so radically—one story, not two, or four, or ten. So what was the story of Jesus that was told around the fire at night, and in the synagogues on Shabbat, and by wells as people drew water, long before the four Gospels were written down in the last third of the first century AD? My hope is that this book will give you a sense of that story. But, I imagine some readers might ask, "Why do we need such a harmony of the Gospels?" There are several good reasons that come immediately to mind.

To begin with, it is high time we did a better job of looking at things from what we know of the first-century Christian perspective, and not the fourth-century perspective (when the canon of the New Testament was settled). I have heard evangelical and other orthodox Christians say that they want to be more like the earliest Christians; well, it's time to live into that in the twenty-first century, especially when it comes to Jesus. The original story that went out from Jerusalem did not come pre-packaged as the four artful and different Gospels that we have in our Bibles. That was a development of the later first century AD. And when the Gospels were finally written, at least two of them were not written by eyewitnesses. I do not say this to critique our Gospels. I love the fact that we have four versions of Jesus' story. Jesus is a man who fits no one portrait—he is too big and complex a historical figure. I simply say this to point out that there was a singular history and a single story of Jesus that existed before there were written Gospels, and subsequently to ask, "What did that story sound like?" I hope this book will give you a glimpse of that story.

Next, we live in the age of atomization and sound bites, and it happens to the good news in church buildings almost every Sunday. We often cannot see the forest for focusing on the individual (albeit very interesting) trees. And when you look in detail at particular Gospel passages, what you discover is a very telescopic, bare bones treatment of Jesus' words and deeds. Doubtless this was originally due, in part, to the need to confine the whole story to one papyrus roll. But even in the case of Luke's Gospel, which is the longest and could just barely be squeezed onto one papyrus roll, we are still left wanting more—more description, more context, more background to the individual stories that make up the one story of Jesus.

What would a more contextual chronicling of Jesus' life, with more historical detail and comment, have looked like? In this book I seek to begin to answer that question. I don't think there should be any tension over this; we need to see the grand sweep of the unified story *and* we need the perspective that the four portraits of the Gospels offer. Just now, it is the former that is neglected again and again in a church which preaches single words, or salient ideas, or tiny passages, and which uses lectionary readings, which means some passages are never heard. There is a need for an overview like this to put the various Gospel pieces together; not to supplant the four portraits of the Gospels, but to scrape off some of the dust that has accumulated on them over the centuries, and allow you to see the vibrant colors in which they were originally painted. What is especially needed is an attempt to show how the Synoptic Gospel portraits (Matthew, Mark, and Luke) fit together with John's portrait of Jesus.

Imagine for a moment that you could hear the story from someone who has heard Jesus tell the story. Wouldn't we want to hear that just as much as we love to hear the later tellings by the evangelists? Who wouldn't pay good money to have been in on that Emmaus road Bible study led by Jesus, where he went through the Hebrew Bible and showed where it referred to him? My point is simple: a good critical probing and blending of the story is as close as we can get to what actually happened back then as a single storyline. Why wouldn't we want to try to do that as a faith venture, not to supplant the four Gospels, but to enhance our understanding of the history behind the four accounts of the one story?

Armed with these reasons, what I have attempted to do here might be called "Ben's Diatessaron," or four Gospels in one, like the effort of Tatian, the early church father. I have stuck as closely as I could to a verbatim telling of the four Gospels, not trying to present a critical edition of the story, with things omitted because of questions of historicity. No, this was an exercise in seeing if one could make sense of the stories as they are, if one combined them all together.

Thus, what you have here is a significant amount of the English texts of these Gospels. I am using the Common English Bible as my primary translation, varying from it only where I have concluded that there is a better rendering, offered from my own translation work. I have also deleted material that was duplicated. It is important to note that, just as the four Gospel writers arranged the individual stories in ways that were shaped by their theological goals, I have arranged the stories to my own ends. Thus, some material may appear to be misplaced, or out of chronological order. I have often combined some of the brief stories, vignettes, and sayings in ways that make sense and flow naturally or logically together. Sometimes this involves a sort of topical arranging of things; at other times, a geographical sorting of the material. I hope that seeing familiar stories in unfamiliar places will help you hear them afresh.

I have chosen not to include the birth narratives, except by way of flashback, and in this regard I am following the example of Mark's work, our earliest Gospel. Of the material which I have added to the Gospel texts, some is interpretive, some explanatory, and some is connective material, tying the stories together.

Let me emphasize once more that no one should conclude from this that I think it is problematic that we have four canonical Gospels, because I do not. I think Jesus was such a complex and important historical figure that even four interpretive portraits is hardly enough. But this book is intended to help the reader put the pieces of the story together in a fresh, meaningful, and helpful way so they may see its range, arc, purposes, and trajectory better. I must stress once more that in the church and in schools, too often, the stories of Jesus are handled only in bits and pieces. This is particularly the way we approach Sunday school lessons and sermons. One hardly ever gets a sense of the whole story in one or two sittings. I hope this effort may go a little way to remedy this problem. New Testament scholar Gerd Theissen's excellent and creative retelling of the Gospel story as a single plot line, *The Shadow of the Galilean*, has been used in seminary classes for more than twenty years. I hope that this book may prove equally as helpful.

The alert reader will also see that I am trying in this portrait to help us understand what the Gospel writers are telling us about the relationship between what we call the humanity and divinity of Jesus. This is a very complex matter indeed, which the Gospel writers approached somewhat differently than the later church fathers. The Gospel writers do not talk about the two natures of the Christ, but they certainly do present Jesus as both human and much more than human—indeed, much more than even an angelic figure. In fact, as John suggests at the very beginning of his Gospel, some of them, at least, were prepared to call Jesus both Son of God *and* God in some sense, without suggesting that Jesus was the same person as the heavenly Father. How does one do justice to this? As you will see, I have intimated in this book that the Son of Man title, which Jesus certainly did use of himself (alluding to Daniel 7) may well provide us with the clue, since the figure in Daniel 7 is not only bequeathed an everlasting kingdom in which he personally would reign, but he is also the judge of the earth, and the object of worship. At least that is how I read that text, and I believe Jesus himself would have read Daniel 7 that way.

I have not tried to psychoanalyze Jesus in this book, but I have tried to tease out the implications of what the Gospels say or hint about the thought life of Christ, and how he viewed himself.

For a critical approach to this subject, please see my older study, *The Christology of Jesus*. I hope the reader will sense both the pathos and the irony in the story, the honesty about the disciples' foibles and lack of understanding, and the mystery of why Jesus said and did some of the things that he did. Most of all, I hope that the reader will, having read this book, see him more clearly, love him more dearly, and follow him more nearly. If that happens, even in small measure, I am content.

Ben Witherington III
Christmas 2013

List of Place Names

Bet Anya	Bethany, or "house of poverty/misery"
Bet El	Bethel, or "house of God"
Bet Hesda or Bet Zatha	Bethesda, or "house of mercy"
Bet Lehem	Bethlehem, or "house of bread"
Bet Saida	Bethsaida, or "house of fishing"
Bethphage	or "house of the early figs"
Gennesaret	The plain on the northwest side of the Sea of Galilee, between ancient Tiberias and Capernaum
Gerasa	A region on the east side of the Jordan river
Hinnom Valley	A narrow gorge curving along the west and south sides of Jerusalem
Jericho	A town just northwest of the Dead Sea
Kefer Nahum	Capernaum, or village of Nahum

Kidron	A dry wadi just east of the old walled city of Jerusalem, separating it from the Mount of Olives. A brook ran through it during the rainy season.
Kinneret	The Sea of Galilee, or the Lake of Tiberias
Migdal	Magdala, or "tower"
Nain	Location uncertain, but in the vicinity of Nazareth in the plain of Jezreel
Netzerit	Nazareth, possibly "branch town"
Qana	Cana
Sepphoris	One of the leading cities of the Lower Galilee, northwest of Nazareth
Yerushalayim	Jerusalem

Premonition

A GENTLE BREEZE drifted over the ridge and cooled the skin of the man seated beneath the ancient, gnarled olive tree. As the breeze dried the beads of sweat on his forehead, he gave thanks to G-d[1] for this sole source of shade high above his hometown, Netzerit.[2] He often climbed the goat path to this spot to gaze with affection at the valley below. And to think. The bleating of sheep and goats reached his ears, as did the faint sound of chisels shaping stone in the quarry of the neighboring town. A pair of sparrows twittered nearby, foraging for food amidst the scrub. As his thoughts coalesced, the sounds merged into the background and his eyes took on a distant look.

---

1. Out of reverence, Jews in Jesus' day used circumlocutions, saying things like "thank heavens" rather than "thank God." Some of them spelled the name of God using a combination of two divine names in order to avoid mispronunciation. I have chosen to use the modern practice of rendering God as G-d to indicate the reverence Jews have for the divine name.
2. In order to give a more Jewish flavor to the story, I have given Semitic renderings of some of the place and personal names.

1

Earlier this morning he had felt a strong urge to get away, to be by himself. The news had reached Netzerit that his cousin John had not only left his community by the Salt Sea, but had gone to the region of the Jordan and was preaching and baptizing people there. A considerable crowd from all over Judaea had come out to see for themselves this man with the air of the ancient prophets about him. The mood here in Galilee was restive; a keen sense of anticipation was in the air. A question was on everybody's mind and on many lips: Was the appearance of this man, John, an indication that G-d was finally about to do something about the ungodly people who ruled their land? Was G-d about to bring an end to the things that, with far too much regularity, made the land unclean?

The man on the ridge—Jesus[3] of Netzerit—knew he had to go down to the river to witness what was happening, and he already sensed that it was going to involve him. And sooner rather than later.

Opening the little bag tied around his waist, he took out some dates and dried figs and began to eat, but his mind was not on his food. Instead, he found himself ruminating once more on what it might mean that G-d had chosen him and his cousin to do something new, something important for his people. Jesus was not yet sure what form his own participation in this new act of G-d would take, nor was the timing of it clear in his mind. He

---

3. There is always a problem when dealing with names in Aramaic and Hebrew that we then translate or transliterate into English. Jesus' real name is Yeshua or Joshua, Mary's real name is Miryam, and most confusing of all, James' real name is Jacob. I decided it would be too confusing and off-putting to avoid all the Anglicized forms of these biblical names, so I have stuck with Jesus and James. But you will find other male and female names closer to the Hebrew and Aramaic original, wherever I thought it would not lead to perpetual puzzlement.

would continue to pray, seeking the counsel of G-d—his Abba—about these things, which was in part why he had come up on the ridge. It was nearly time for late afternoon prayer anyway, but he also wanted to focus, to be ready, and so needed to get away from distractions. Jesus had a strong sense that he was about to reach a crucial turning point in his life. He had always resolved to do nothing without depending on his Father, listening intently for guidance so that he would always live firmly in the center of G-d's will. So he had come here to pray. To listen. And to prepare himself for what lay ahead.

The noise from the quarry ceased, as the men laid down their tools to pray. As Jesus' lips moved, joining the distant quarry workers in reciting the 145th psalm, he gazed out across the valley. He could see yet more buildings rising in the new town called Sepphoris. The rate at which Herod Antipas' new city was rising from the ground was truly remarkable. Nearly a third of the male population of Netzerit and nearby villages like Qana was employed in one way or another, so that Herod would soon have his new city, this so-called Ornament of the Galilee. Stone masons, carpenters, water carriers, artists, painters, caterers, and many more were working from dawn to dusk, seldom resting—except, of course, on the Shabbat.[4] The people of Netzerit had never seen construction on this scale or with this speed. The town talked of little else. Jesus' own family had been contracted to do some of the carpentry work, which meant that Jesus had been involved in Herod's project, as had his brother James.

As James' face came to mind, Jesus could not help but think of Joseph, their father, whom James so plainly resembled. It

---

4. The Hebrew word translated as "Sabbath" in English.

had been nearly two full years since Joseph died, leaving Jesus, the eldest son, in charge of the family business. Everything was going well, the construction work in Sepphoris doing more than just putting food on the family table, yet Jesus felt a knot in his stomach. He knew that the time was drawing close when the shape of his life would be completely changed. It was almost time for him to leave home, an event that would create enormous problems for his family. To begin with, they would certainly feel the loss of his wages. Then there was the fact that Jesus had his doubts about whether James would be able to handle taking responsibility for the family's affairs. Was he ready to take over the family business? Would he be able to arrange good matches for their sisters, given that there were few young men in Netzerit to choose from? Most painfully, Jesus' apparent abandonment of his family would bring shame upon them all. Jesus had never discussed these things with James, but now, most certainly, he would have to.

"But I must talk to Mother first," murmured Jesus. "She at least will understand that I must go." His thoughts drifted back through the years. How many times had Mary told him about that first trip to the City of David, Yerushalayim? Just a few days after he was born in the house of his relatives in Bet Lehem, they made the journey to the capital city for his ritual circumcision as an eight-day-old male. Mary had told him of an old man named Simeon, there in the temple, who gently took Jesus from her arms with the praises of G-d on his lips. This man spoke prophecy over her firstborn son, saying that he would be the cause of the rise and fall of many in the land of Israel, unveiling the secrets of human hearts, and that he would be "a sign spoken against" by those who would reject him.

But what could all that mean? wondered Jesus. Prophecies by their nature are enigmatic, requiring much thought to puzzle them out. But that was not all. Simeon had also told Mary that "a sword will pierce your heart as well." Was he talking about the scandal that would ensue when Jesus suddenly left his mother and younger brothers and sisters? Was he talking about the disappointment, sadness, and pain she would feel when he left them? It was not clear. Nothing was completely clear.

The sound of construction reached his ears as the men took up their tools once more. Jesus took a swig from his water skin and returned to his thoughts. Surely his sudden departure wouldn't come as a complete surprise to Mary. After all, she had seen plenty of warning signs that his life must be different from that of his brothers and sisters. There had been that other trip to Yerushalayim for Passover, when he had just come of age. Unbeknownst to his family, who had begun the journey back to Netzerit, he remained in the temple precincts listening to the sages and scribes teaching there, and asking them questions.

Surely his mother would remember his response after she and Joseph told him of their desperate search during those three long days. Had he not said to her then, "Did you not know I must be in the house of my Father?" Jesus had not intended it as a rebuke, but when Joseph hung his head, he realized how the words must have stung. Yet one more reminder to Joseph that he was not the actual father of his eldest son. Jesus had no wish to shame his parents, so he stopped what he was doing and submitted to their authority, trudging home with them all those long dusty miles back to Netzerit. Yet it had been exciting to talk to those learned men, and all the way home he thought about what it would take for him to grow in wisdom as well as in stature, so that he would be fully ready to be involved in his Father's business.

But perhaps Mary would not remember this as vividly and clearly as he did. After all, that had happened more than fifteen years ago. He also knew that she was still grieving the premature loss of her husband. Not a day passed without her stopping by the back room to run a lingering hand over his workbench. Joseph had not been an old man. If that beam had not fallen upon him during the construction of one of the buildings in Sepphoris, Jesus would still be seeing the creased lines of his mother's smile instead of the lines of grief so clearly etched in her face. Jesus could not picture her marrying again, despite the encouragement of friends and neighbors. She had loved Joseph so much, and the family's finances were secure without the need for her to be remarried. But still, the neighbors talked.

Jesus smiled to himself, knowing that he was also the subject of such gossip. After all, had he not refused offers of marriage three times himself? Not only the fathers of the prospective brides had been incensed. Most of the town made it clear that they also wondered just who Jesus thought he was, refusing such gracious offers and opportunities. So now here he was, twenty-seven, unmarried, and about to do something which he feared would further add to his family's burdens. The words of the prophet Isaiah came unbidden to his mind: "a man of sorrows and well acquainted with grief." These were the things Jesus pondered as the sun began to slide toward the far horizon.

Lost so deeply in thought and prayer, Jesus did not hear his little brother Joses slip up behind him, and he was startled when that familiar little voice called out, "Jesus! Come home to supper! Mother says it's ready now." Getting up from his spot below the tree, Jesus rose and smiled at Joses. He tousled his hair, and took the small outstretched hand Joses offered to him. Together they headed back down the ridge toward their small house below. Joses looked up to and depended on Jesus, especially since Joseph's death. How could he ever explain to him and the rest of the family what he was about to do? Would they ever forgive him? Indeed, would they ever understand such a drastic departure from village life? He feared not. He knew that tomorrow he would have to muster up the courage to talk to Mary.

2

A Difficult Conversation

MARY WATCHED AS Jesus pushed the food around his bowl, and knew something was amiss. He was clearly preoccupied with something and not his normal jovial self. He had seemed distant as he took his place at the head of the table, almost distracted as he said the prayer of thanksgiving over the bread, breaking it and passing it to each of them. She caught his eye, and he looked away quickly. She turned her attention to her own food, and pondered the change in her firstborn. He was a good son and had faithfully led the family since Joseph's death. What could be troubling him? Could it be the news about John that caused this change? She would have to ask him later.

The rest of the evening passed quietly. Jesus put the youngest two girls to bed, singing psalms to them until they fell asleep. Afterward, Mary approached him, a small hand lamp flickering, casting shadows in the lines of her forehead, concern clearly evident in the ghostly light. She whispered, "Let's go out into the courtyard, so I can listen to what is on your heart." Jesus heaved a sigh of relief, and offered his mother a grateful smile. She knew him so well, had always been able to sense his moods. He realized that tonight was the time for the talk they needed to have, rather than waiting for morning. Stepping outside the house, they walked around the large olive press which took up most of the space in the courtyard, and sat down on the far side.

Jesus looked into the face of his mother, the most beautiful face in all the world to him. He gathered his thoughts and took a deep breath. "Mother, do you remember when I was twelve and we went up to Yerushalayim for Passover, and you thought I was lost?"

Mary threw her hands in the air. "Remember? How could I possibly forget? It is every mother's nightmare, losing a child. When we realized you were missing, I berated myself all the way back to Yerushalayim for not double-checking to see if you were with our relatives when we set out for home. The crowds were huge. I just thought you were with your cousins. I trusted you."

"I know, I know." A look of concern crept across his face. "Do you remember what I said when you found me?"

She held his gaze. "Yes, yes, I remember. You said something about needing to be in your Father's house. It struck me as odd at the time, since we were returning to our home here in Netzerit. And . . ." She paused, then wiped the tears that had sprung suddenly to her eyes. "And I remember that Joseph—he of blessed memory—took it hard. Almost as if you had rebuked him."

Jesus leaned in close, and spoke earnestly. "I never intended it that way, Mother. I was just trying to remind you that there was a calling on my life, one that you yourself had told me about, long before I was twelve."

"I understand, my son. But your father and I were both distraught at the time. We had been looking for you frantically for three days. Surely you can understand why I said what I did."

"Of course, Mother, of course. You were worried. I understand. But I don't bring this up to remind you about the past, or to pick at old scabs. Mother, you know I love you. It is never my intent to hurt you." He looked down at his feet, kicked at a small pebble, then brought his eyes back up to his mother. "But there is something I must tell you."

Mary's face wrinkled with concern. "What? What is it?"

"It begins with another question. Do you remember what the synagogue elder used to say about our town from time to time, when he would tell us the story of Netzerit?"

Concern wrinkled Mary's brow, as she was clearly puzzled by Jesus' question. "What do you mean? What are you asking?"

"What is the meaning of the name, 'Netzerit'?"

"It means something like 'branch village.'"

"But what does that *mean*? Why is it important?"

Mary snorted. "Well for one thing, it means that no matter what the Judaeans may say about our village, we *are* connected to King David. We are connected to the stem of Jesse, as the prophet says."

"Exactly, Mother. This may not be the city of David, or the place where he—or I—was born, but it is the place where many descendants of David, the 'shoots of Jesse,' settled here in the north." He took both of her hands in his. "Mother, this is difficult for me to tell you, but I feel it is time for me to begin to live into this calling on my life. I am a descendant of David. I am a son of David. And what I believe Abba is saying to me now is that I must go and be with our cousin John, and see what G-d is doing there. Perhaps I can help John in some way."

Mary shook her head. "But the family . . ."

"It has been two years since Joseph died, and James is old enough to serve as the head of the family. I believe he can take care of the family business in my absence. Would you not agree?"

There was silence for a moment, as Mary paused to wipe fresh tears from her eyes, shaking her head slowly as emotion welled up from deep within her. "I have always known this day would come. But that does not make it any easier, now that it is here. Certainly you must do what you feel G-d is leading you to do. But you and I both know that it will be hard for those you leave behind. And for you, wherever it is that you go." She grimaced. "You know tongues will wag in this little village. They will say you have shamed your family. They will accuse you of abandoning your family when we still need you. Such talk is bound to come, you know, and we will bear the brunt of it when you are away. That stigma will follow your brothers and sisters for a long time. It will affect their futures."

"Mother, I promise I will come back, at least to visit. I will show them I still care about my family and my friends here. But as you well know, there are some in our town who do not think too highly of me anyway. You remember how they taunted me when I was a boy?"

Mary's face grew distant. "Yes. They called you, 'son of Mary.'" Her eyes focused on his face again. "'Son of Mary,' they used to say. They threw their belief that Joseph was not your real father in your face. Trying to shame you. To shame me." She shook her head sadly.

"How vividly I remember that."

A thin smile came to her lips. "But Joseph put a stop to that soon enough. He told those boys' fathers to keep their sons' mouths shut." Her head lifted with pride at the memory, and the smile broadened, even as her face softened. "Your father was such a good man. Even before G-d told him the truth about the child I carried in my womb—the child he knew was not his—he refused to shame me. He resolved to divorce me quietly. Until the angel came."

She looked deep into Jesus' eyes. "You were *always* the child of Joseph's heart, even if not of his body."

Jesus' eyes glistened. "I know, Mother."

"But do you remember what I told you about how I came to carry you in my womb?"

"Who could forget? To be told I had come from G-d through you!" Jesus laughed. "I don't suppose that those who slandered you when you were pregnant with me thought for one moment that you could be the one written about by the prophet Isaiah."

Mary began to recite the prophet's words, her eyes distant, her voice full of wonder. "'Listen, every one of you in the royal family of David. A young woman is pregnant; she will have a son . . .'" She turned back to Jesus. "No, my son, I don't believe they recall Isaiah when they think of me. But what will they think of you, when you leave? How shall I answer their questions?"

"I have thought about that. Tell them the same thing you will tell my brothers and sisters. That I have simply gone to visit my cousin John so that I can verify what people are saying about him. That will satisfy them, and—of course—it also happens to be true."

"That answer will only silence the talk for a while," Mary said apprehensively.

Jesus could see how very tired, and emotionally drained, his mother was. He helped her to her feet, bringing the conversation to an end. He hesitated for a moment and then wrapped his arms around her, feeling her warmth and smelling the scent of her hair. Would this be the last time they shared such an embrace? Jesus allowed his mother to cry quietly on his shoulder for a few minutes, neither of them sure of what lay ahead.

As he held his mother, Jesus whispered, "What was it you told me when I was a child? The best thing for any child of G-d to ever do is to do G-d's will on earth, as it is in heaven?"

"Yes, I suppose I did say that. But it doesn't make this parting any easier," lamented Mary. She looked up into his face. "But know that I will always be proud of you for following the calling on your life."

"And Mother, whatever happens to me from now on, know that I will never forget to honor you and pray for you and care for you, till the day I die." He gave her a kiss on the cheek. "And now, we must both get some sleep."

Walking back into the house, Mary blew out the flickering flame of the lamp which sat on the little table Jesus had made long ago. They headed off to their corners of the house to lie down until sleep finally overtook them.

Waking with a start, Jesus looked out of the window and could just see the slightest hint of dawn beginning to creep up the hill toward his house. Through the window to his left, he saw the light of the stars fading overhead. Morning was inexorably on its way. But what had pulled him so suddenly from his sleep?

"It was my dream," murmured Jesus to himself. He sat up, resting his chin on his knees as he pondered what he had seen. A human-like figure, descending on a cloud and being given all power and authority by G-d to rule forever on the earth, following long aeons of beastly rulers and empires that had dominated the world and even ruled over G-d's people. So vivid was the dream, it felt as though Daniel's vision had been given once more, only this time to Jesus himself!

But what startled Jesus most was that when he had looked closely at the face of the figure, the *bar enasha*, the "Son of Man," it seemed eerily familiar. The face in the dream looked just like the reflection he had seen in a bucket of water his mother drew from the well the night before.

3

Migdal and Qana

ON THE NORTHWEST corner of the sea called Kinneret or Tiberias sat the little village of Migdal, between Kefer Nahum and Bet Saida. All three of them were fishing communities, and business was booming at this time of the year. One could always tell when things were going well, as the number of soldiers at the tax collectors' booths increased, ensuring that Rome, Herod, and—of course—the tax collectors, got their share. However, the usual grumbling in Migdal about taxes was usurped by a new topic of conversation: their village's beautiful new synagogue, complete with a stone reading table decorated with floral designs and a carved image of a menorah. The pride in the little village had been palpable since the synagogue was completed that summer.

High above Migdal, in the hills that led up to the cliffs of Arbel, was a cave. A woman sat in its entrance, covered in dust from head to toe. She was not an old woman, but her face made it clear that life had not been kind to her. Abandoned, she had no one to talk to, save herself.

"'Unclean' they say, 'unclean.' But who are they, the lords of life, to judge me?" she asked of no one in particular. Her hair was disheveled and she had covered herself in dirt for protection from the relentless sun, as well as the vermin that crawled around in the cave. Her name was Miryam, named for the prophetess, the sister of Moses. But she was not honored among men as her namesake had been. No, she had been cast out of the village because they suspected she was possessed by unclean spirits. There were also stories that men had used her for their pleasure. But that was not true: some had tried, all had failed. Despite her small frame, Miryam had a wiry strength and a piercing voice, when she needed it. She defended herself with shrieks and kicks, fighting her assailants off. Her parents were dead and her only brother had left town looking for work, leaving her, well and truly, alone.

Her mind drifted back, as it so often did, to the day a few months earlier when she came to live in this cave. A day she would never forget. A young woman of twenty-five, all alone, she had sought to enter the new synagogue early on Shabbat, seeking help and cleansing from G-d. But suddenly, as had happened before, she blacked out, fell down, and began to writhe on the new mosaic floor, spittle foaming from her mouth. The president in charge of maintaining the synagogue at once called for several townsmen to help drag her out of the holy place. Clearly she was not well and, evidently, unclean—perhaps even possessed by demons.

Miryam awoke some time later lying outside the graveyard, just beyond the village boundary stone. Bruised from the fall, bewildered to find herself there, she had stood up to head back down the hill to where she lived. But as she turned to go, the watchman of the graveyard approached her. "You cannot come into the village or the synagogue again. You are possessed, unclean, cursed by G-d. We cannot have you here, contaminating

others in our village, much less contaminating the holy place."
He held out a small bundle. "Here are your clothes and things.
Take them and go. Away from here."

She accepted the bundle, but whispered, "Where? Go where?"

"Anywhere but Migdal. You're not welcome here ever again!"
The man crossed his arms, clearly indicating he would not allow
her to return to the village. She staggered up the hill, stumbling
as tears streamed down her face.

She passed the shepherds and their flocks, barely registering
their presence. And that day, she discovered the small cave in
which she now sat. In one of her more lucid moments, she was
able to ask the shepherds where she could find spring water, and
a few olive and fig trees had provided her with food—at least for a
season. She was given bread to eat as well, in exchange for sewing
some garments for the itinerant shepherds and goatherds. But
apart from this sporadic contact with fellow humans, Miryam
lived alone. The spider and the scorpion, the birds and the wild
animals were her sole companions. Cast out, cast down, casting
about for food and life, she lived in maddening and utter isolation.

The town of Kirbet Qana lay off the beaten path, like Netzerit
itself. No major road went there, but the east-west trade route
was close enough. Like many villages in the Galilee, there was a
growing unease, an increasing fear that something was wrong,
terribly wrong. The response of the town folk, like those who
lived in the community by the Salt Sea, had been to dig more
mikvahs—baths—for ritual cleansing. And more and more people
were availing themselves of them. There was illness in the land,

uncleanness in the land, foreigners in the land, demons in the land—though it was supposed to be G-d's special land, a holy land. It did not augur well for the future. The people asked themselves why G-d was punishing his people with leaders who so clearly failed to deal with their problems. Obviously, there must be significant sins for which they needed to repent: cleansing was required.

One such indicator of uncleanness was the presence of the Herodians—officials sent by Herod Antipas—in the towns and villages. Ostensibly sent to supervise the collection of taxes, they were really an observing and monitoring presence, Herod's spies in Galilee. Even in Qana, one of Herod's court officials, a *basilikos*, now lived in their midst.

But that was not all.

It was feared that this court official might also be connected to the Roman army. After all, his name, Decimus, was not Jewish, but Roman. As both a court official for Herod Antipas and the ears of Caesar's governors in the region, this man had received no welcome when he tried to ease his way into village life. His presence made their skin crawl, one more reason for the increase in visits to the mikvahs. The word on the street was that he had adopted his servant, making him his son. This, some townsfolk found odd; others, reprehensible. Obviously, the man cared little about tribal identity, blood lines, and proper genealogies. What kind of person adopted a slave anyway? And the fact that this man worked for Herod said it all. No faithful, G-d-fearing Jew would do that.

There had been no enthusiasm when Herod Antipas came to rule the Galilee, the territory bequeathed to him by his father, Herod the Great. The Herodian line was not fully Jewish in any case, Idumean blood running in their veins, for they were Edomites. Any who knew their people's sacred history knew that there was bad blood between Edom and Israel. The Israelites took perverse pleasure in the prophet's words, "Jacob I have loved, but Esau I have hated," and they thought that was rationale enough for their animus against the descendants of Esau, the Edomites.

And then there were all the pretensions the Herods brought to the region, their aspirations to be like the great Hellenistic rulers. This, they tried to accomplish with their massive building projects. Antipas had already created a major hue and cry with his first significant enterprise, the city of Tiberias by the sea. Not only was it named after an unclean emperor, but Herod had shown such little regard for Jewish sensitivities that he built the city on top of a Jewish graveyard. He had to pay the Jewish settlers to move there, since it was a place of uncleanness. Incredible!

The resentment and anger toward Antipas had been simmering for a long time, and occasionally it boiled over. The Zealots were always looking for opportunities to stir up anger against the supporters, sycophants, and officials of Herod—officials like Decimus. And yet there was another side to Decimus. For Decimus *was* a G-d fearer, a person learning to be observant of Jewish ways and customs.

On this particular morning, however, the conversation in Qana was not about the Herodians. The village was abuzz with talk of the coming wedding of two of their residents—Jacob and Esther—the children of two prominent families. Relatives would be coming from as far away as Kefer Nahum for this long-awaited festive occasion. Relatives such as cousin Mary, from Netzerit, who on this day had walked the dusty road to Qana to help her niece plan for the wedding, now just a few short months away.

On the way there, Mary had thought back over her conversation with the children about Jesus' departure. Breaking the news did not go as well as she had hoped, but about as well as she expected. No doubt there would be more questions when she came home. James was furious, and could not accept Jesus' decision, even after Jesus gently tried to explain to him the importance of his going to be with John.

A weary smile creased Mary's lips. At least she could take her mind off her troubles by thinking about the joy of the coming wedding day. She wondered if Jesus would return for this special family occasion. Life never said "please," it just kept going and changing. *But*—Mary wondered as her smile faded—*will the changes be for the better, for our family?*

4

John the Baptizer

JAMES, THE SECOND eldest son—and quite feisty because of it—had made it abundantly clear he did not appreciate having this responsibility dumped in his lap so unexpectedly. He told Jesus that he had been thinking about getting married soon, and this would delay those plans for quite some time. At least he had not discussed the matter with the father of the woman he had his eye on, so there would be no embarrassment. Jesus knew that James had always labored in his shadow, envying his precociousness and the fact that as the firstborn son, Jesus was entitled to the lion's share of the inheritance—even though he was not actually a son of Joseph. This James found increasingly hard to swallow.

He had not even been placated when Jesus told him that the inheritance of the eldest would now go to him. James had refused to believe the family whisperings about Jesus being the Promised One, G-d's anointed of the line of David. From his point of view, though Jesus was now twenty seven, none of his actions suggested he might be the long-awaited Messiah. For James, Jesus' lack of interest in the kind of violent revolt the Zealots were engaged in, his lack of interest in withdrawing to join the community by the

Salt Sea, and his meek payment of taxes all pointed away from the possibility of him being the Messiah. Indeed, his whole approach to such troubling matters seemed to be one of *non*-resistance. Surely the Son of David could not be expected to act like this? It certainly didn't meet James' expectations or understanding of the ancient prophecies. True, Jesus occasionally did things that could be considered remarkable, but then so had the prophet Elijah. And that hardly made Elijah the Messiah, now did it? At most, his brother might be some kind of healer or prophet, but he showed no signs of engaging in public ministry or confronting their repugnant rulers, as even Elijah had done.

Jesus knew all of this, that his brother did not know what to make of him. He was a mystery. Thinking back on these things as he drew close to the river, he sighed.

He came near the spot where his cousin stood in the river, and the sight stirred something deep within him. On the far shore of the Jordan stood several hundred people, all listening to John, moving forward, pressing in on one another to get a better look at what was happening. And the crowd was not just made up of the rural poor, as Jesus might have expected. Along with the fishermen, vinedressers, and day laborers were Pharisees and scribes, Herodians and Levites. There were even soldiers—part of Pilate's auxiliary troops—standing next to elders from synagogues. Jesus saw women and children, grandfathers and grandmothers, all seemingly compelled to come out to the wilderness to listen to John, to be baptized, and then to go away in a different condition.

It had been a long time since there had been a prophet like John in Israel. His very presence suggested to many that the fullness of time might well be at hand, and the Messiah would finally come to save his people. Dressed in a camel's hair outer garment, with long, unkempt hair and a beard, John looked like everyone imagined Elijah to have looked in days of old. His skin dark brown from long days in the sun, his body lean—if not gaunt—and his voice powerful and deep, John mesmerized those who came to hear him. And he spared no one from his words of warning. No official could curry favor with John, and most of them feared his power over the crowds, the ordinary, pious Jews who would follow such a leader wherever he led them. On this very day, John had baptized dozens of people, and dozens more were camping on the opposite shore in preparation for tomorrow's baptisms.

It had taken Jesus longer than he expected to find John. He had traveled more than a day, following the road alongside the Jordan into Judaea and down toward Jericho, before finally reaching a spot across from Aenon, near Salim, where he was told John could be found. John had chosen this spot, no doubt, because there was plenty of water here, unlike further north in Galilee where the Jordan could scarcely be called a river; there, it barely formed a stream by late summer, when there was no rain at all.

As the sun began to set, Jesus watched John walk out of the river and continue up the slope, away from the crowds, followed by his disciples. Jesus decided to wait until morning to approach him. He knelt by a small pool, took a long drink, and stretched out his blanket on the ground. Filled with anticipation, he lay on his back looking up into the stars. It was hard to go to sleep. He was on his way now, things were in motion: he could feel it. Even when he prayed to G-d, his Abba, before finally falling asleep, his mind was distracted by a thousand thoughts.

What would happen in the morning would prove to be a surprise for both John and Jesus.

5

Jesus' Baptism

JESUS WOKE SLOWLY from a deep sleep. He opened his eyes and looked up. Not a single cloud in the sky, and the only break in the blue was a lone bird that circled high overhead. What kind of bird was it? Too far away to tell. Still, Jesus found it a comforting presence, an unknown bird, a harbinger of an as yet unknown future.

Rising, and going over to the spring, Jesus dusted himself off before washing his hands and face. He filled his water skin, and then unwrapped the few figs and olives that remained in the little bag around his waist. He considered the meager meal before him, then knelt for a brief morning prayer to G-d. "Abba, today as on all days, I need your guidance. And by the look of it, my daily bread, too."

Jesus stood up and smiled, but his senses were tingling, telling him something very significant was going to happen this day. He decided to wade across the river to the far shore, where John's disciples stood. He would engage some of them in conversation and learn what he could before approaching his cousin. The things he had already heard made him understand why the authorities might well object to what John was doing—offering forgiveness for sins quite apart from requiring any sacrifice in the temple in Yerushalayim. *That would displease many people, and cut into the profits of the priests if it continues,* Jesus mused.

If people could repent of their sins, be baptized, and be reconciled with G-d and his people—without making the long journey to Yerushalayim and spending much of their savings on one of the unblemished animals for sale in the courtyard—one could see how some would view this as a threat to both the temple economy and the priests' authority, especially that of the high priest. Prophets often operated on the margins of society and were seen as a threat to the ruling figures, kings, and priests. And consider the way John dressed and preached! Having presented himself in Elijah's garb, he could only expect the sort of response from the authorities that Elijah received.

But John was not hiding at the Salt Sea, nor running to Mount Horeb. He was standing here in the Jordan, in plain sight, inviting one and all to come, repent, and be baptized in preparation for the judgment of G-d that was about to fall on a wayward people.

It took Jesus quite some time to wade upstream through the crowds to where John was baptizing, in order not to disturb him. Jesus had memories of visiting Elizabeth, Zechariah, and John as a boy. Jesus' cousin was just a little older than him, and he remembered John as being restless and full of energy, as well as full of righteous indignation at the spiritual state of Israel. He had always admired John's zeal for all that was holy. The land indeed needed purifying, the people in the land needed purifying, and at the time of Jesus' visit, John was already contemplating joining those at the Salt Sea. These pious Jews repeatedly cleansed themselves as they awaited G-d's final victory and eschatological judgment to fall on Israel, particularly on Mount Zion because of Herod's opulent temple, which had been constructed at the cost of many human lives. Jesus remembered his uncle Zechariah telling him of the day he was inspired to prophesy about his own son, the prophet to be. His words for John had affirmed that,

> "You, child, will be called a prophet of the Most High,
> for you will go before the Lord to prepare his way.
> You will tell his people how to be saved
> through the forgiveness of their sins.
> Because of our G-d's deep compassion,
> the dawn from heaven will break upon us,
> to give light to those who are sitting in darkness
> and in the shadow of death,
> to guide us on the path of peace."

John's mission, then, was to prepare for what would come after him, to call G-d's people to repentance in order that they might be cleansed and saved. But who was the One that John was preparing the way for? What was this "rising sun" coming from heaven to guide people in the paths of peace? Zechariah could not say, but even as a boy Jesus remembered and thought about his own mother's words, "You have come from G-d." Now, it was imperative that he go to his cousin, and perhaps find out from John what his own destiny might be.

By the third hour of the morning, Jesus was standing on the far side of the Jordan. It was already a hot, blistering day, and he was thankful that his cloak was still cold and wet from the crossing. He introduced himself as John's cousin, Jesus, to the man standing next to him. The man embraced him and said his name was Andrew from Bet Saida. He was a fisherman from the northwest shore of the Kinneret, and had become one of John's followers.

Looking around at the crowds, Andrew said, "It has been simply amazing to watch what has happened over the last several weeks. The crowds have gotten larger and larger, coming from both Galilee and Judaea and even places like Perea, Nabatea, and Idumea. The word has spread like wildfire that G-d is preparing to do something major for his people and that everyone had best prepare for it, whatever it is. We must renew our commitment to our G-d, and receive forgiveness of sins." Andrew spoke with enthusiasm, his tanned face beaming with the confidence of having already seen remarkable things.

Then he lowered his voice. "But I tell you now, John is in no way currying favor with the authorities. Indeed, he has warned them, most severely of all, about the coming judgment they face. I can tell you, they are none too pleased to hear that. There is even talk about John being taken captive." He looked around at the crowds. "But at this moment there are simply too many supporters of John around for them to try that here. If they have any sense, that is."

"Tell me about the baptisms," said Jesus. "It seems to be something different than just the regular ritual ablutions, something more than simply going into the mikvah."

"Yes," said Andrew, nodding enthusiastically. "That's right. It's something like the initiation rite of the Salt Sea community, a one-time rite of passage, in this case a once-for-all rite of repentance and forgiveness of sins. But it only *prepares* the people for the coming judgment and mercy of G-d. It doesn't *convey* either of these things. John says it is a prophetic act, a warning. The immersion is a symbol of death and burial of the old self, cleansing from one's past."

Andrew paused to look out at John, standing in the river. "And there is something else. The sacred Scripture which the

Essenes at the Salt Sea took as their theme is from the prophet Isaiah. I'm sure you know it: 'the voice of one crying in the desert, "Prepare the way for the Lord, make straight in the wilderness a highway for our G-d."' John has taken this as his own theme, his own calling. Only he disagrees with the Essenes on the interpretation of the text. He believes he is to call one and all to prepare, not just holy people who retreat from society and purify themselves, but everyone, even Gentiles—even Gentile soldiers! And just look at what is happening!" As he said this, he stretched out his hand in the direction of John and the surrounding crowd.

"The young, the old, the wealthy, the poor, the Herodians, the priests, men, women. G-d is doing something dramatic in our day." Andrew turned to Jesus. "Could this be the sign that Messiah is coming soon? Is John the Elijah-like prophet Malachi talked of, who prepares for the Day of G-d?" His face suddenly shone. "I believe it is, and many others among John's disciples do as well. John makes it clear he himself is not the Messiah, but he knows he is preparing for something momentous to happen, for some great intervention of our G-d. Let's move closer so we can hear his words."

As Jesus and Andrew eased through the crowd, they saw that John had stopped baptizing and appeared to be staring at some people standing on the far shore.

Jesus walked slowly, picking his way through John's disciples, many of whom stood mesmerized by the sight of so many people entering the Jordan. Andrew led him to a good spot where they could both hear, down a path to a little sandbar next to the river. Jesus saw that all eyes were focused on John, who did indeed cut a remarkable figure in the blazing sun. He looked like a wild man, with his tousled hair, his scrawny frame, and his garment of animal skins. There were reports that he had taken to eating the insects of the desert—locusts—with a little wild honey to wash them down! There could hardly be a sharper contrast between John and some of the Pharisees and Herodians on the far shore, attired as they were in their immaculate robes, even here in the wilderness. John continued staring at them for a long moment, and then began to exhort them in a loud voice.

"You children of snakes! Who warned you to escape from the angry judgment that is coming soon? Produce fruit that shows you have changed your hearts and lives. And don't even think about saying to yourselves, 'Abraham is our father.' I tell you that G-d is able to raise up Abraham's children from these stones. The ax is already at the root of the trees. Therefore, every tree that doesn't produce good fruit will be chopped down and tossed into the fire."

Andrew turned to Jesus. "If looks could kill . . ." Jesus, seeing the expressions on the faces of the Pharisees, nodded in agreement. Andrew sneered. "You won't see any of that lot getting their pretty robes wet in the river with John. No, look there: it's tax collectors and soldiers. John tells them how to change their lives. What they must do before G-d's judgment falls on them."

They watched as John baptized those immediately around him, one after another. Then he addressed the crowd, speaking once more in a deep, clear voice:

"I baptize you with water, but One who is more powerful than me is coming. I'm not worthy to loosen the strap of his sandals. He will baptize you with the Holy Spirit and fire. The rake he uses to sift the wheat from the husks is in his hands. He will clean out his threshing area and bring the wheat into his barn. But he will burn the husks with a fire that can't be put out."

Andrew turned to Jesus again. "He keeps deflecting attention away from himself, keeps denying he is G-d's Sent One. But it's so clear that he is indeed G-d's prophet, preparing for the great and terrible Day of the Lord. It's all very confusing, but it's also breathtaking, to think that we might be living on the edge of the end of days!"

Jesus was silent for a while in reflection, as John returned to baptizing. Andrew looked at Jesus but could see that he needed to be left to his own thoughts. After several more minutes, Jesus suddenly stepped into the Jordan and started wading forward. John's back was turned, so he did not see Jesus silently and steadily moving toward him. Now standing in water up to his waist, Jesus reached out and touched the prophet, saying gently, "John."

Hearing the voice, John jerked around abruptly. He appeared shocked, but before he could speak Jesus said, "Baptize me, John." Looking incredulous, John protested, "It is you who should baptize me, for you have come from G-d!"

Jesus smiled at his cousin. Then Jesus' face stilled, as if listening to an inner voice. His eyes widened and then he said, "Still, let it be so, to fulfill all righteousness." John paused, looked deep into Jesus' eyes, and then nodded his assent. Placing his arm on Jesus' back, he held Jesus' two hands with his other arm. Very slowly he lowered Jesus completely into the water and then lifted him back out again.

Time stood still.

Jesus looked up, and his eyes grew wide. A single cloud had formed in the sky, which was suddenly rent in two, and people started at the loud clap of thunder that accompanied it. But as Jesus later told his disciples, he did not hear thunder, but instead a voice from heaven that said, "You are my beloved Son; with you

I am well pleased." And there was more than just the voice. Jesus would tell them that he received power from on high on that day, the mighty Spirit of G-d falling upon him and remaining on him. In fact it was only after the Spirit descended that he heard the voice from heaven. The Spirit heightened all of Jesus' senses, and he could hear the voice of G-d so much more clearly from then on. Indeed, from that day forward, he felt empowered, equipped for the task before him. Yes, this was the time. His decision to leave his family, however painful, was part of his Abba's plan for him. The experience at the Jordan had been the confirmation he needed: not merely a confirmation of who he was, but also that it was time for him to begin to fulfill his calling, to engage in the work he had been sent to do.

But as suddenly as Jesus had come to John, he left and waded out of the Jordan on the Judaean side of the river. Once on the shore, he walked rapidly away so as not to draw any further attention to himself. It was as if he had an urgent matter to attend to, a pressing task to complete.

Andrew, who had seen the whole encounter, was left to ponder, muttering to himself as he stroked his beard: "I wonder who that man *really* was. And why did John say that Jesus should have baptized him?"

6

Temptation

JESUS FOUND HIMSELF stepping deeper into the wilderness, almost with a sense of compulsion. Everything had changed with his baptism—his work would begin in earnest now. The words the Father had spoken reverberated in his head, and he wondered aloud, "But what sort of Son am I to be, Abba? And how will I demonstrate that to your people, that I *am* your beloved and only begotten Son?" He needed clarity, a vision from G-d. In the past he had fasted and prayed many times, and as he thought of doing the same now, images of Moses and Elijah on the mountain came to him, and he suddenly realized that this fast must be lengthy: forty days of preparation.

On the eve of the last day of his fast, Jesus sat in the shade of a rock. His tongue was swollen, his belly was tight, and he barely had the strength to crawl out from the shade to drink from the stagnant pool of water nearby. His whole body ached, and when he looked down at his withered limbs he shuddered. "One more day,"

he muttered. He turned to prayer once more, increasingly sensing that the vision would come, that his task would become clear.

On the fortieth day, he slowly woke up and pulled his thin covering closer around him. The sun was already quite high. As he looked up to determine the hour of the day so he could say morning prayers, he suddenly saw a blinding flash of light that seared his eyes. Hesitantly opening them again, he saw a figure—an angel of light, surely! Was his fast about to end? Would this messenger give him the vision from G-d?

But as soon as he heard the sibilant hiss of this figure's words, he knew this was not his Father's messenger. He heard the mockery and the challenge in the voice as well as the words: "*If* you are the Son of G-d, then turn these stones into bread." Jesus glanced at the stones scattered close by, and his stomach groaned. How was he to respond to the challenge? Surely it was a test of his character, of his identity, and he must not fail it. Yes, he had access to the Spirit's power and, heaven knows, he was sorely tempted to produce some food. After all, had not G-d miraculously provided manna for Jesus' ancestors in the desert? And he *was* hungry. But his identity—not bread—was the issue here. What kind of Son would he be? What purpose would his power serve? If he was indeed going to fulfill all righteousness like a true Israelite, then to get through this trial, Jesus needed to rely on the Word of G-d and the Spirit of G-d, the same two resources available to any pious person. He pushed himself slowly to his feet, and faced the vision of light that stood before him.

Through cracked lips, his voice rasped, "It is written, 'People don't live by bread alone, but by every word that comes from G-d's mouth.'" As he spoke these words, his mind returned to the generation that had wandered in the wilderness. Daily, they had received manna, teaching them to rely on G-d to provide the necessities of life. Even as his stomach growled in protest, Jesus determined to do what Israel had not. Praying for daily bread showed that one relied on G-d. G-d had led Jesus into this fast, and G-d would be the One to break it.

Without warning, the vision changed. Now Jesus saw the temple precincts and, utterly disoriented, he found himself standing on the pinnacle of the corner of the temple, over-looking the Kidron Valley. The voice came again. "If you are the Son of G-d, then you can surely throw yourself down from here; for it is written, 'He will command his angels and they will lift you up in their hands so that you will not strike your foot against a stone.'" Now the voice coming forth from the light was hurling Scripture back at him, like a weapon. But Jesus, in his heart, did not believe he had been called to use his power gratuitously, or for his own protection, or to prevent his experiencing the painful consequences of poor human choices. And why was this angel urging him to rely on angels for his rescue, when he need not put himself in danger in the first place? He looked down to see the throngs in the temple courtyards, and had a vision of himself descending gently from on high to land safely in their midst. What would such a demonstration of power in this place—the very heart of his people's life—do for his standing among them? Then he knew the nature of this test. With a smile, he turned to address the figure again.

"On the other hand, it is written, 'You shall not put the Lord your G-d to the test.'" Jesus felt deep gratitude for the presence of the Advocate with him, strengthening him to oppose the schemes of the Adversary. But relief was fleeting, as the vision changed yet again. Now Jesus seemed to be standing upon Mount Hermon, the tallest mountain anywhere near Galilee. From here he could see without limit in all directions. The Adversary moved in for the kill. "All this I can give to you, if you will just bow down and worship me."

Barely able to stand, Jesus found the weight of this temptation almost overwhelming. The thoughts came rushing in. *How easy it would be to free G-d's people, if suddenly I was the ruler of this world. I could accomplish all I wanted for G-d's people, immediately and at no cost.* Except the cost that would come with betraying his Abba, his G-d, just as his people had done over and over again throughout their history. Now understanding fully who this angel of light was—the ruler of this fallen world—Jesus set his face like flint, and summoned what strength he had left to reply, "Away from me Satan, for the Scripture says, 'You shall worship the Lord your G-d, and him only shall you serve!'" What kind of beloved Son would he be if he betrayed his Father, the only proper object of human worship, by worshiping such a lesser being as the Adversary? No matter *what* the Adversary could offer.

As quickly as the vision had come, it disappeared. Jesus found himself drenched in sweat and ravenously hungry, still lying in the dirt on top of the mount he had ascended to pray forty days earlier. Despite his hunger, it was his exhaustion, his need for rest which prevailed. The last thing he remembered before falling soundly asleep was the presence of some other beings of light—angels—attending him. He must have passed the test. G-d had come to his aid and he had been faithful. As he was closing his eyes, he thought to himself, *Henceforth, I must live as, and present myself to others as, the Son of Man: truly human and yet also more than human, like the Son of Man in Daniel. I must constantly remind myself to live within my human limitations, limitations of time and space and knowledge and power, the limitations of mere mortals. Only so, will the sons and daughters of humankind be able to follow me and imitate my pattern of life. Only so, will I avoid the trap of appealing to one or another set of preconceived notions of what "the anointed one," the ultimate son of David, must be and do. Only so, will G-d prevail and save his people from their sin.*

Looking for Learners

WHILE JESUS RECOVERED from his ordeal, he thought about the task before him. John's preaching and baptizing might well be serving as a wake-up call for many Galileans and Judaeans, but Jesus didn't find himself reflecting on a mere amendment of life. No, he thought about the time in which they were living. John, in much the same pattern as the prophets of old like Amos, warned of coming judgment and the need to repent in preparation. But Jesus' vision of what was about to transpire involved more than this. It would be good news rather than an emphasis on impending doom. He understood that salvation is not merely rescue from judgment; it is also healing, restoration, transformation—*shalom*—G-d's wholeness.

When he thought of the time they lived in, Jesus could not help but think of the end of days. Yes, he believed the time was right, the time was fulfilled, and he must act at this propitious juncture in history. He thought about the eschatological Jubilee—when those in bondage would be set free, when those in debt would have their debts cancelled, when those who were diseased or unclean would become well and whole. In short, Jesus thought of healing and help—even of new birth.

The coming dominion of G-d on earth would involve saved, healed, and whole persons. But this meant that people, even Israel's lost sheep, had to actually change within. This was not merely a question of changing religious practices or the occasional change of moral behavior; it was inner change. This heart transformation was necessary, since it is from the heart that hatred, lies, envy, lust, and all the horrible things that distort and ruin human life and community proceed. As Jeremiah said, G-d's instruction has to be inscribed by his Spirit on the human heart, and not just on tablets of stone and rolls of parchment. All this necessitated a dramatic divine intervention before the dominion could come on earth; a new covenant written on the heart must precede a new people living in the land.

And, Jesus mused, *wouldn't that old fox Herod Antipas be surprised to learn what sort of person will live and thrive in G-d's dominion—the meek rather than the manipulative, the pious rather than the powerful, the givers rather the takers, the lovers rather than the violent?* Such was the vision of Isaiah and other prophets, and such was the vision of Jesus.

But how would Jesus get the message out that the least, the last, and the lost could become the most, the first, and the found? How would he get the message out that the dominion of G-d was not only for the privileged classes if they repented and lived a different, more generous life? How would he convey that the poor already had an advantage, for their daily experience necessitated that they must trust in G-d and not unrighteous mammon or possessions? How would his family, friends, and neighbors understand a new message which placed the emphasis on internal transformation rather than external cleansing? After all, mikvahs were being built everywhere in Galilee. The people knew something was wrong in the land, but they did not see the solution. Yes, proclaiming the message would be a challenge, but he was ready and equipped to begin.

As he walked down the mountain, Jesus resolved not to waste time but immediately to recruit some learners, those who would be willing to follow him, to learn his message, and to emulate his pattern of life. They would help him proclaim the good news to everyone in both Galilee and Judaea, and not only there, but also in Samaria and the surrounding regions. Yes, this good news was for the Jew first. But as the prophets said, it should be for the whole world, for Father Abraham had been blessed to be a blessing to all peoples, not just his own family. It was time for an Israelite without guile to fulfill the mandate given long ago to G-d's people, to not only be succor to their own kin, but also to be a light unto the nations.

Jesus pondered who to call as his learners. *I must recruit a diverse group*, he said to himself. *It must involve both men and women. Oh, there will be an uproar about that, but the dominion is for everyone.* But he decided to start with men. He thought that some of John's followers would listen to him and follow. They were already excited about the new thing G-d was doing among the people. So it was that Jesus returned to the Jordan to talk to Andrew and a few others. *Perhaps Andrew could help in the recruiting*, thought Jesus, as a plan began to form in his mind.

The journey back to the river took little time, only an hour or so, but John had moved upstream and some hours passed before Jesus found him and his disciples once more. As Jesus was approaching, John looked up and pointed at him, saying with excitement to his disciples, "Here is G-d's Lamb, who takes away the sin of the world!" Jesus had meant to spend some time with John and talk about what he was seeing, but immediately two of John's disciples came over to Jesus. Andrew reached him first and asked, "Teacher, where are you staying?" His instinctive response was, "Come and see." So Jesus took them back across the Jordan to the spot where he had camped earlier.

"We must go back to Bet Saida and Kefer Nahum," said Andrew. "My brother Simon will want to hear about this!" Jesus took note that both of these men were young, barely twenty. The second had not spoken yet, but already Jesus could tell there was something special about him. He seemed warm, friendly, with an air of genuine piety, someone who would be dedicated to the work ahead.

"What's your name?" asked Jesus.

"Lazarus," said the small man, "or Eliezer, as some would have it."

"And where are you from?"

"Bet Anya, near Yerushalayim. You must come and visit my home and meet my sisters." He paused, looking down for a moment before snapping his head back up. "Do not listen to those who say we are unclean because my father, Simon, was a leper. My father has passed away and now I am the head of our household, which has been thoroughly cleaned, as the priests can attest. I have to go back to Judaea now, but please, you must come and visit us and share your plans and vision with us." Jesus noticed how sensitive the young man was, concerned that Jesus might hear bad things about his family and faith. He immediately liked Lazarus for his openness, directness, and deeply devout nature.

"I will," Jesus promised, "but first, I am going with Andrew up to Galilee. I will recruit some learners there first, but I will come to Bet Anya." Jesus and the young man embraced and parted company, but Jesus knew something significant would develop in their budding relationship. G-d was already steering people to him for the work of ministry.

The journey to Kefer Nahum was undertaken on the far side of the Jordan, traveling north on the king's highway. There were many on the road that day. Jesus saw camel drivers heading south for Petra, the mysterious Nabatean capital, to sell their animals. There were also pilgrims on the way to the temple, who would cross over the Jordan at Jericho and head up the steep and winding Jericho road to Yerushalayim. There were soldiers heading north, perhaps to Syria to rejoin their legion.

Along the way Jesus struck up conversation with two men from Tyre. They were money changers who had just come from Yerushalayim, where they had delivered Tyrian shekels and half shekels to the priests. These were necessary so that pilgrims could exchange their own coins for the ones normally used to pay the temple tax, the tribute money, and to make offerings at the temple treasury.

"So, you're saying that people can now even buy animals and exchange money in the temple precincts themselves?" Jesus asked.

"That's right," said one of the money changers. "The Sadducees and the priests have concluded that that's the best way to increase the revenues of the temple complex, and help pay for the ongoing construction there, no doubt with Herod's encouragement." He laughed aloud. "They will get more revenue that way, than when people buy animals on the Mount of Olives or in Bet Lehem or somewhere else."

"But surely that must interfere with those praying in the outer court, righteous Gentiles and others?" said Jesus.

"Yes, the noise in that courtyard is remarkable," said the tall man in the black robe who was the older of the two Tyrians. He laughed derisively. "I doubt anyone could even hear G-d if he *did* happen to answer a prayer, unless of course it involved shouting! I believe the priests also have some personal plans for their newfound revenues. They do love keeping up appearances."

"This does not bode well for the future of that place," said Jesus, his face turning grim. "What was it the prophet Jeremiah warned about a temple becoming a den of thieves?"

"Or at least a din of noise," replied the old Tyrian with a wry grin. "As for thieves, I ran into a few in the temple precincts. One of them tried to avoid paying me my commission for transporting the coins. Jeremiah's prophecy must be coming true right now."

The many building projects of the Herods were ongoing, and taxes were required to fund them. Herod the Great's temple in Yerushalayim itself was still a work in progress after many years under construction. Herod had been dead for a quarter century or so, but still the building went on in both Judaea and Galilee, as well as elsewhere. There were problems with all this, thought Jesus, but it *did* keep many ordinary Jews gainfully employed.

Andrew listened to this and other exchanges as he and Jesus headed north, but his mind was more focused on his brother Simon. Simon was not merely a fisherman by trade, he was an avid fisherman by choice. It might be hard to convince him to leave his nets and come join Andrew in following Jesus. How could he be convinced, especially when this summer the fishing business had been such a success, so profitable? Before he knew it, he and Jesus arrived at the place in the road where they had to take the left fork and cross the Jordan just south of the Kinneret. This was the last chance for an easy crossing. After that they would walk past Tiberias and on to Kefer Nahum and Bet Saida, and find Simon and the others by the sea.

"Where shall we stay tonight?" Jesus asked Andrew.

"Of course you must stay with us," he replied. "Or, if we do not reach Bet Saida before dark, we can stay the night at Simon's mother-in-law's home in Kefer Nahum. We should be there before the sun has set." He looked at Jesus out of the corner of one eye. "You know, it's going to take some convincing to get Simon away from his boats and nets. Both his body and his will are strong."

Jesus smiled at Andrew. "Tomorrow we must take the rock from the water, rather than the water from the rock," he said enigmatically. Andrew had no idea what Jesus was talking about, but he replied like a good learner, "Yes, Master, whatever you say. But we must eat and rest tonight first."

And with this the two men picked up the pace and approached the Jordan once more. They crossed over and walked for a while. When Jesus reached for his water skin to ease his thirst, he realized he had not refilled it when he had the chance. He held the empty skin upside down and shrugged at Andrew. "Not to worry," Andrew said. "There's a spring with the clearest water you ever saw, just up beyond that village."

They climbed the hill for some distance. As they drew near the spring that came forth from the limestone cliffs, Jesus saw someone sitting there alone, eagerly gulping down the water, and washing her hands and face over and over again. Jesus walked over slowly to fill up his water skin, kicking loose rocks to alert the woman to his presence rather than risk startling her.

Quite to his surprise, when Jesus came near to the spring, the woman who had been sitting there began shrieking at the top of her voice, recoiling in horror as Jesus approached. In an inhumanly loud voice she screamed, "Do not torment me, Son of David. Have mercy upon me!"

The face of the woman was contorted beyond all recognition, and she was shaking all over. Drool came from her mouth. It was clear that the woman was possessed, and Jesus knew that this alarming reaction was not that of the woman so much as that of the one—or ones—who had taken control of her mind and heart. Holding his right hand out toward her, Jesus felt a surge of power race through his body, and then he said in a voice that brooked no opposition, "Leave her! Now! And never return again! In the name of the Almighty, I cast you out!" The woman gave another ear-splitting scream, before convulsing and rolling on the ground. Then, silence—a long silence into which Jesus spoke gently, "Shalom to you. May G-d's wholeness now prevail in your life."

At first the woman stared into the distance, barely present to the two men. Andrew looked on cautiously, quite shaken by what he had just witnessed. As he watched, tears quietly began to stream down the woman's face. Jesus continued to speak gently. "What is your name, daughter of Abraham?"

A feeble voice barely croaked, "Miryam, Miryam of Migdal."

After sitting with her for a few minutes until she had fully come to her senses, Jesus said, "Come daughter of Abraham, let us go down to your village below, and I will vouch to the local elder or priest that you are once more in your right mind." Handing her his walking stick, as she was still shaking and unsteady on her feet, they headed down to the village below. Every now and again the woman glanced sideways at the man who had just delivered her from her torment.

When they reached the synagogue, Jesus asked for the president. He came out, and immediately shrunk back from Miryam. "What are you doing here?!"

Miryam moved closer to Jesus, who addressed the president. "This woman has been released from the forces that oppressed her, and she is to be restored to her life in the village, as Torah requires." The president shifted his attention to this stranger, who had an unmistakable note of authority in his voice. Then he looked closely into Miryam's face for a long moment before saying, "Is this true?"

"Yes," she said, trembling slightly. "It is true. I am at peace. I am whole."

"And how is this possible?" he demanded.

"The power of the Most High has done this," answered Jesus.

"But who is responsible for this?" demanded the president.

"I am."

When the president did not respond, Jesus said, "Tell the village elders that the one who was lost to you has been found. And rejoice for what G-d has done. Rejoice that the dominion of G-d is in your midst!"

With that, Jesus turned and strode away from the village, Andrew at his heels. The president of the synagogue stared at his back, before turning back to Miryam. As he saw the peace written large in her expression, his own face softened. "Come, child, let us go to the village square and announce the good news!"

8

Simon

JESUS SAT BY the lake, skimming stones across the placid water. It was early morning and only the fishermen had been out on the lake thus far, but with meager results, the air and the water being so still. Jesus had enjoyed a second quiet night at the house of Simon's mother-in-law in Kefer Nahum, and had slipped out early to think and pray by the seashore.

His first exchange with Simon a couple of evenings earlier had gone well enough, and Simon introduced Jesus to his family in what he soon came to know as the fisherman's usual effervescent, loud manner. Simon was a man of definite opinions, with a very low opinion of tax collectors and the others who worked for Herod Antipas. At the same time, he was suspicious of ultra-holy men as well—prophets, priests, sages, and the like. *Is he suspicious of me?* wondered Jesus.

Simon was a believing Jew, but not always a scrupulously observant one. At the end of the family meal, and after some hours of conversation, Jesus had come up to his host and said, "Thank you for your kind hospitality. I have a name for you— you will be called Cephas," which is the Aramaic word for "rock."

46

At the time Simon merely laughed a bit, thinking Jesus was yet another peculiar prophet of some sort. But it was a nickname he didn't mind having. And yet why had Jesus said, "You will be called Cephas"? When, and by whom?

The word about the healing of Miryam of Migdal had spread quickly. Indeed the townspeople in Migdal, Bet Saida, and Kefer Nahum had talked of little else yesterday. How had a woman full of unclean spirits suddenly regained control of her life, suddenly returned to her right mind and a state of cleanness? She had told all who would listen, "It was Jesus of Netzerit who healed me." And now here he was back on the shores of the Kinneret. Simon's mother-in-law had told the neighbors, and so when Jesus turned around from gazing at the sea, there was a small crowd of people, not wanting to bother the healer, but still hoping for some help, or at least some healing words.

Within fifteen minutes the throng grew much larger, and as newcomers arrived, those at the front began to crowd Jesus. He looked over his shoulder and saw Simon and Andrew rowing two small boats back toward the shore where he now stood. Simon groused that they had caught next to nothing after several hours of early morning fishing.

Jesus waded into the shallows, and reached for the boat as it drew up to the shore. "Simon, can you take me on board, please? I'd like you to row a bit offshore so I can speak to all these people without them pressing in on me." Simon shrugged his willingness, though it was clear he was in a poor mood after the paltry catch.

Jesus began teaching the crowd in parables—one after another. Some of these were just brief analogies, others more like comparisons by means of a brief story, but in each case Jesus introduced the parables by saying they were about the coming dominion of G-d. The one that stuck in the mind of Simon and Andrew, naturally enough, was one about a fishing net.

"The dominion of heaven is like a net that people threw into the lake and gathered all kinds of fish. When it was full, they pulled it to the shore, where they sat down and put the good fish together into containers. But the bad fish they threw away. That's the way it will be at the end of the present age. The angels will go out and separate the evil people from the righteous people, and will throw the evil ones into a burning furnace. People there will be weeping and grinding their teeth."

The story made Simon uneasy, and he began shifting back and forth in the boat. What pile of fish would he end up in, when the angels came to sift humanity? He was not sure, and the more he thought about it, the more uncomfortable he became. The problem with prophets and sages was that they not only comforted the afflicted, but they often afflicted the comfortable as well.

After teaching for about half an hour, Jesus said to Simon, "Put out into the deep waters, and let down your nets for a catch."

Simon was exasperated. "Master, as you know, we have worked the better part of the night, and have basically caught nothing worth keeping. Yet, if you say we should try again, I will let down the nets once more just to please you. But don't expect much!"

They rowed out quite a distance and then turned the boats. Simon and Andrew stretched out the nets between the two boats and began rowing in tandem back toward the shore, hoping to catch a few fish by trawling. Andrew was anxious, wondering what Simon would think if there was still no catch. But suddenly, without warning, the nets began to fill with fish. So many fish swam in that the nets were bending under the weight and the boats started tipping toward each other.

Frantically, Simon called out to a couple of his friends on shore, who were standing next to their own boat, ready to row out to them as they drew close to land. All the while, Jesus sat quietly in the back of the boat, watching all that was happening with a wry smile.

The newcomers helped pull Simon's and Andrew's boats close together, and the nets were dragged up into them. Both boats became so full of fish—and so many different kinds!—that they were on the verge of sinking. When Simon saw this, his eyes grew wide, and a blend of fear and awe gripped him. Wading through the fish to the back of the boat, he fell on his knees before Jesus. "Please go away from me, for I am a sinful man!" The two other fishermen who had rowed out to help were equally stunned by the catch. Their names were James and John, the sons of an old fisherman named Zebedee.

Jesus turned to Simon. "Do not be afraid, Simon. From now on you will be fishing for and catching human beings, a much more slippery and elusive creature." Simon felt a sick feeling in his stomach. He realized he had been "reeled in" by Jesus, and that hereafter he would do whatever Jesus commanded. As they were pulling their boats ashore, Andrew looked at the nets and said, "I guess we won't be needing these for a while."

"I guess not," said a suddenly serious and somewhat glum Simon. He was not the kind of person anyone would call contemplative, and so his silence spoke volumes as he, Andrew, and the Zebedee boys sorted the fish, placed them into small containers, and then hauled them back to their houses.

When they got back to the house of Simon's mother-in-law, Simon's wife came to the door to tell him that her mother was stricken with a fever, and she didn't want to let anyone in for fear of spreading the disease. As soon as Jesus heard about it, he said to Simon, "Let me see her for a moment. I can help." It took some convincing, but Simon persuaded his wife to let Jesus into the house. The sun was going down and Shabbat was coming, so there was some urgency to the situation.

Entering the small sleeping room where Simon's mother-in-law, Naomi, was lying, Jesus could tell from how greatly she perspired that the fever was high. Standing over her, he reached down and took her hand in his own. She looked up at him through glazed eyes as he began to gently pull her to her feet. She allowed herself to be raised up, and she knew instantly that the fever had left her. For a moment she stood there in amazement, then turned away quickly and said something about needing to prepare supper for them all. She walked into the cooking area at the back of the house, as if nothing out of the ordinary had happened! A small crowd had gathered outside the door, but Jesus sent them away so the family could be in peace. They needed to eat before going to the Shabbat service at the synagogue.

The local synagogue ruler, Jairus, came to the house to ask Jesus if he would do them the honor of teaching at the service. Jesus gladly consented. Jairus had heard about Jesus from Andrew just that morning. When dinner was finished, the whole family got cleaned up and went. But when they arrived, there were already many townspeople crowding into the synagogue, far more than usual. Many had heard Jesus in the morning; others had heard about the big catch of fish. Some were there desperately seeking healing. Jesus had an eager audience, and he did not disappoint.

After the introductory remarks of Jairus and the reading of a scroll of one of the prophets, Jesus sat down, as was the custom of teachers, and began to proclaim, "The time is fulfilled and the dominion of G-d is at hand. You must repent, turn your lives around, and believe in the good news of the salvation and healing that G-d has brought into your midst." As he continued to teach, the crowd began to murmur. Why was he not citing other teachers?

Jesus' apparent miracles and his telling of parables evoked memories of the prophets of old, especially the famous northern prophets, Elijah and Elisha, who were deeply revered here in Galilee. He seemed to know things about what G-d was doing now, in their midst, and what beckoned from the near horizon—hence the exhortation to repent. This message sounded a lot like John the Baptizer, except that Jesus kept telling them they must believe the good news. *Since when was the coming of judgment "good news"?* they wondered. But Jesus also spoke of salvation on this day.

Quite unexpectedly, a young man worked his way up to the front of the congregation to where Jesus was sitting, and began screaming at Jesus. "What have you to do with us, Jesus of Netzerit? Have you come to destroy us? I know who you are, the Holy One of G-d!"

As those nearest to the young man drew back, Jesus replied in a strong and angry voice, "Shut up, and come out of him!" The young man convulsed and there was another loud cry, then a brief whimpering, and then the young man called for his father.

He sat quietly for a moment on the synagogue floor, recovering. Then he stood up and walked out of the synagogue, apparently well. Remarkable! Both the teaching and the exorcism left the congregation in stunned silence at first, but then they began talking among themselves, asking one another, "What is this? A new teaching with authority, and he commands even the unclean spirits and they obey him!" There would be no way to keep all of this quiet, and indeed the word spread like a brush fire in a dry olive grove.

Jesus realized that he needed to get out of town, and quickly. The problem was clear: he wanted to spread the good news of G-d's salvation breaking into their midst, but the profound physical needs of so many people were so pressing that the healings and the exorcisms spread by word of mouth throughout Galilee, while his teachings seemed to be considered of less importance. The call to repent, to receive the good news, and to be transformed would fall on deaf ears—ears which seemed only to want to hear about miracles, and eyes that only wanted to see signs and wonders. Jesus knew how wide a gulf lay between physically healing someone, who would then go on to live and die as all people do, and changing them not only for this lifetime but also for eternity. He knew there was a huge difference between an amazed crowd, and a believing, changed community.

Very early the next morning, while it was still quite dark, Jesus got up and left the house of Simon's mother-in-law. He went up into the hills above Kefer Nahum to pray. Things were moving quickly, and Jesus wanted to hear what his Abba would have him do now, in light of current circumstances. He prayed for a while, and then heard voices coming up the path to where he sat. Simon, Andrew, and the sons of Zebedee had found him. Simon said, "Everyone is searching for you!"

Jesus held Simon's gaze for a moment before saying, "Then let us move on to some of the neighboring towns, so I may proclaim the good news there also; for that is what I came to do." And so it was that Jesus went to Migdal, and Bet Saida, and Korazin, proclaiming the coming dominion of G-d. After a week and more of travel, Jesus told his disciples that he needed to go to Qana, for the time had come for the family wedding. He also longed to see his mother. Several of the disciples decided to go with Jesus, even though he promised that he would return to Kefer Nahum afterward.

9

To Qana

AS THEY WALKED the road to Qana, Andrew found his eyes straying regularly to Jesus. It had not taken him long to notice some noteworthy differences between Jesus and John the Baptizer. Jesus was no ascetic, nor did he dress in spartan clothing or shun the unclean. Indeed, he seemed not only to enjoy spending time with people who were ritually impure, but also those who had lapsed in their morality. When Andrew asked about this, Jesus told him that he had not come to call the righteous to repentance, but the sinners, the lost sheep of Israel. And as it turned out, it was indeed the least, the last, and the lost who loved Jesus and followed him around. Many of them, to Andrew's mind, were like stray puppies looking for attention, sustenance, and a helping hand. This made Andrew nervous, because he knew what some of the Jewish authorities, especially the Pharisees, would say about it. Jesus was obviously not concerned about making people comfortable, including his disciples. No, his concern was focused on those who wanted the cure for sin-sickness that he offered, those who were "born again"—or who "turned and became as a child," as Jesus put it.

They walked due west, passing the cliffs of Arbel and crossing the main north-south road, and then began to wind their way up the footpaths that led to Qana. Andrew now turned his attention to one of the traveling companions who had recently joined them. He and the other fishermen, Simon, James, and John, were equally uneasy about the presence in their midst of the man named Matthew, or Levi as he was sometimes called, coming as he did from a Levitical or priestly family. But Matthew was no priest. He was a reviled tax collector. His recruitment by Jesus struck them as strange, even remarkable.

Matthew had stepped away from his tax booth to join the crowd on the day of the big catch of fish, and Andrew spotted him then and saw the gleam in his eye. No excuse now for the Zebedees and the Bar-Jonahs not to pay their back taxes! But Matthew was excited by more than the thought of revenue. Convinced immediately that Jesus was a remarkable person, he looked upon him with deepening awe. And so, when Jesus approached Matthew's tax booth later that day and invited him to be one of the disciples, he didn't hesitate, and walked away from everything he had worked toward in the past.

Jesus was the first holy man who had ever given Matthew the time of day, let alone asked him to "come and become my follower." To top it all off, Jesus had suggested they dine together that night, and Matthew readily agreed, inviting his friends—tax collectors and other "sinners"—to the meal. Naturally, the fishermen were not pleased at all with this development, as it made them look foolish and caused all kinds of gossip in their little village. What kind of holy man could Jesus be, if he banqueted with those people? It was a scandal! And yet, there was no denying the power of G-d they had witnessed as Jesus healed people in the village.

Still, Andrew thought, *traveling with Matthew certainly was awkward.* To Simon, he was their bloodsucking enemy, a traitor who collected taxes for Antipas' many building projects, and even now Andrew could see a dark expression on Simon's face as he regarded the man. But Matthew, for his part, walked along with a broad smile, asking Jesus question after question. As a tax collector, he could both read and write. Perhaps the Master saw value in his ability to write down the parables, riddles, and beatitudes that he taught, which Andrew had seen Matthew doing the previous evening. Who knew? At least he was outnumbered by the fishermen, who figured they could keep him in line if necessary.

As they approached Qana, Andrew glanced at Philip, the other resident of Bet Saida that Jesus had recruited, beside the Zebedees. Philip actually knew someone in Qana that he wanted to introduce to Jesus, a devout student of Torah named Nathan'el, meaning one "given by G-d." They walked through the village gates, and Andrew looked around at this "place of reeds," the name given to the village because of the marshy areas surrounding the spring. Qana was very religious, full of mikvahs and cisterns to collect water for purification. It was only about four miles from Netzerit, and several of Jesus' relatives lived there. They were proud that though small, the village had produced some renowned scholars and a few scribes. Jesus asked Philip to lead them to the home of Nathan'el.

Philip ran ahead to Nathan'el's house and knocked on the door. Nathan'el opened it and Philip, scarcely able to contain his excitement, said, "We have found him about whom Moses and the prophets wrote. Jesus bar Joseph from Netzerit!"

Looking incredulously at his friend, Nathan'el retorted, "Surely not! Can *anything* good come out of that little undistinguished town up the road, much less the Messiah himself?"

Philip's only reply was, "Come and see." By this time, Jesus and the others had arrived in front of Nathan'el's small house, and as soon as Jesus saw him he said, "Now here is an Israelite in whom there is no deceit, no dissembling."

Dumbfounded, Nathan'el said, "How do you know me?"

"In my mind's eye," said Jesus, "I saw you sitting under your fig tree in the little courtyard behind your house, studying a Torah scroll before Philip called you."

Nathan'el's eyes grew big, as he realized that Jesus had both insight and spiritual sight. He blurted out, "Teacher, you must be the Son of G-d, the King of Israel so long awaited and hoped for!"

Jesus laughed. "Do you already believe in me, just because I told you I saw you under the fig tree? Trust me, you will see greater things than these! Amen, amen,[1] I say to you, one day you will see heaven opened and the angels of G-d ascending and descending upon the Son of Man."

This odd remark silenced not only Nathan'el, but also the rest of Jesus' followers. Nathan'el wondered about this Son of Man. Was Jesus speaking about himself in the third person? That in and of itself was odd. Obviously, Jesus' words brought the story of Jacob and the angels to mind, the story of Bet El, the gate or house of G-d. But could Jesus really be saying that he

---

1. The term "amen" is often translated "truly" in English, not least because Jesus used the term in an unusual way—before he was going to say something important and significant. Furthermore, it was normally the response of another person, when someone told the truth. Jesus testified to the truthfulness of his own words in advance of speaking them.

himself was that same juncture of heaven and earth, the place where G-d's presence could be found? Surely that was the temple in Yerushalayim. Was Jesus claiming that he himself was the locus, the house, the temple of G-d where the Holy One of Israel dwelt? Such were the questions rattling through the mind of this scholar of the Scriptures, as he invited the six men to come in and enjoy some figs and wine before they headed over to the house of Jesus' relatives.

The conversation at Nathan'el's house was friendly, and the disciples were glad for some refreshment and food after their long walk. Jesus excused himself, saying that he must head further into the village to find his mother and see how the preparations were going for the wedding and the feast that would follow that afternoon.

He found his mother standing in a courtyard, giving instructions to a couple of servants who were setting up the *chuppah*, the wedding tent that was the central focus of the ceremony. She looked up to see her son leaning against the wall, watching her in her element, and ran to meet him. Mary wrapped her arms around Jesus' waist and leaned her head on his chest. Then she looked up into his face and said, "My son, I have missed you so much! How glad I am to see you! We are behind in all the preparations—what else is new? It is always this way with a wedding. Everybody is coming. I just hope we have enough food!" Her eyes went to a pile of amphorae, or two-handled jars, in the corner of the courtyard. "And enough wine."

She looked back into Jesus' face and smiled. "Wait until you see your cousin Jacob, and his bride-to-be, Esther. They look wonderful. Jacob is with his father. Can you believe they are still haggling over the bride price with Esther's father? Hopefully that will end soon. The bridesmaids are getting nervous, because they're supposed to lead the procession here. That's supposed to happen just after sundown, and we have only an hour or so more before then."

Mary blurted out all of this and more before Jesus could even greet her, so delighted was she to see him. She had heard the reports filtering back to Netzerit that there had been miracles, healings that Jesus had performed, and that he was now a teacher with followers. This did not entirely surprise her, as she had always known that he was special, known that he was different from her other children. James, on the other hand, dismissed these reports, calling them "exaggerations." He was still angry with Jesus for leaving home so abruptly and leaving him to look after things.

Jesus patiently listened to his mother prattle on for a while. She was worried, and he knew it. He told her he had to get back to his followers, but that he would return quickly, and that naturally, they would all come to the wedding as well. Mary's brow wrinkled, and she glanced once more at the supply of wine. "Oh my, how many extra guests does that make?"

"Seven, counting Nathan'el, whom I think you know, since he is a local boy."

"Oh yes, the young Scripture scholar with the precisely cropped and curled hair, who always wears the black-and-white prayer shawl." She lowered her voice conspiratorially. "Behind his back, the town calls him 'the holy boy,' he is so intent and intense in his study of Torah. He will make a good disciple for you, my son."

"Yes Mother, I know," Jesus said as he walked away. "He is entirely earnest and honest."

When he got back to Nathan'el's house, Jesus sat down in the courtyard where the disciples were still chatting and eating figs. "Well," he said with a smile, "as usual, they are behind schedule in getting this wedding started, so perhaps I can tell you a story about a wedding."

"Please teacher, we would love to hear your words," said Nathan'el.

Sitting up straight, Jesus put his hands in his lap and began. "Let me tell you a parable about the end of the age. At that time the kingdom of heaven will be like ten young bridesmaids who took their lamps and went out to meet the groom. Now five of them were wise, and the other five were foolish. The foolish ones took their lamps but didn't bring oil for them. But the wise ones took their lamps and also brought containers of oil. When the groom was late in coming, they all became drowsy and went to sleep. Then, at midnight, there was a cry, 'Look, the groom! Come out to meet him.' All of the bridesmaids got up and prepared their lamps. The foolish ones said to the wise ones, 'Give us some of your oil, because our lamps have gone out.' The wise bridesmaids replied, 'No, because if we share with you, there won't be enough for our lamps and yours. We have a better idea. You go to those who sell oil and buy some for yourselves.' But while they were gone to buy oil, the groom came. Those who were ready went with him into the wedding. Then the door was shut. Later, the other bridesmaids came and said, 'Lord, lord, open the door for us.' But he replied, 'I tell you the truth, I don't know you.'"

Jesus looked intently at his disciples before saying, "Therefore, keep alert, because you don't know the day or the hour."

Nathan'el was the first to respond. "So are you saying we cannot know the timing of when the Messiah will come? But are you not he? Haven't you already come?" Over in a corner, sitting on the edge of a cistern, Matthew picked up the tools of his trade and began taking notes of what Jesus was saying.

Jesus quietly responded. "This parable is not about the beginning of the dominion on earth, but rather its consummation. While there are signs now that the dominion is breaking into your midst, the culmination of all things will come at an unexpected time. It is one thing to talk about the beginning of the end, the beginning of the dominion of G-d on earth; it is another thing entirely to talk about its consummation."

No one dared to ask Jesus a further question. It was not what they had expected to hear. "But enough seriousness," said Jesus, changing the mood. "It is time for us to arise and go to the wedding and celebrate!"

10

Water and Wine

THE WEDDING FEAST was the biggest celebration of the year for this small village. Practically everyone in town was invited, and those who were not showed up anyway, after last-minute invitations were extended out of an overflow of joy. And of course, Jesus' disciples were there too. These latecomers tested the resourcefulness of those who served the food, as they scrambled around trying to meet the demand. The wedding ceremony had been beautiful, and now it was down to the important business of toasting the bride and groom, eating, doing some more toasting, telling tales, and the like.

Standing in a corner of the courtyard, sipping on a cup of wine and observing the proceedings was Decimus, the *basilikos* who lived in Qana as the official representative of Herod. He had always been quiet and discrete, and no one had any real cause to complain about his presence, at the wedding or in town. He was on the road a good deal, his territory stretching from Qana to Kefer Nahum and points north.

True, some said Decimus was a Roman soldier, a centurion in disguise, but it seemed more likely that he was a Semite of some sort, not a pagan. It was hard to tell, though, because Herod and Pilate both had auxiliaries working for them who had been recruited from the local population. Clearly this man was not of Greek or Roman descent, for he sometimes attended synagogue in Qana, and when he was in town he seemed respectful of some Jewish customs. Indeed, he had a mikvah at his house.

Jesus slipped across the courtyard to meet the man, and was soon in intense conversation with him. He felt a tug on his arm, and he turned around to find Mary standing there.

She stood on tiptoe to whisper in his ear. "We are about to have a hospitality disaster. They've run out of wine."

Jesus looked at her with surprise and said somewhat curtly, "Woman, what's that to you and to me? Don't you know my hour has not yet come?" Mary's lips trembled as she gazed up into her son's eyes. She knew that Jesus had to do things in his own time, at his own pace, following G-d's plan and guidance. But wasn't the fact that he had brought half a dozen burly men along—uninvited, mind you—part of the problem? Still, as she looked at Jesus' face, a sly smile appeared on his lips, which seemed to send a different message than the one his words had conveyed. She guessed Jesus did not want to become the center of attention at the wedding, but she sensed he would do something.

Turning to the wine steward and his servants, who were standing close by, Mary said, "Do whatever my son tells you to do." Over against the inside wall of the courtyard stood some large stone jars. Each could hold twenty to thirty gallons. They were jars meant for purification water, for the various ablutions necessary when a family practiced the Levitical laws of cleanliness. They had undergone heavy use before the feast, and were now practically empty. Jesus said, "Go to the spring outside and fill each of the jars full of water."

Without hesitation the servants ran to the spring and began bringing bucket after bucket of water, filling up the jars to the brim. This process took about half an hour, during which time even the wedding party themselves ran out of wine, and the toast-master looked anxiously about for the wine steward. Just when he was about to panic, Jesus told the wine steward, "Draw out some of what you find in that first jar, and take it to the toastmaster, the head steward." When the cup was given to the toastmaster, he looked into it, took a sip, and looked again, stunned. He had no idea where this new wine had come from, but it was the best he had tasted all day. Usually they served the best wine first, when the palate was more discriminating; later, they would serve the cheaper or more watered down wine. Something was amiss here.

Calling the bridegroom over, the toastmaster said to him, "Jacob, everyone serves the good wine first, and then once the guests have had their fill and are less discerning, one serves the inferior wine. But you have kept the good wine until now!" Jacob could only smile and say that he didn't know why that was the case. He looked at the wine steward, who in turn looked at Jesus in a meaningful way. Jacob followed his eyes, and nodded. One more unexpected thing in a day full of surprises.

But Jesus' mother and disciples knew what had happened, because they had been there for all of it, beginning with the conversation between Mary and Jesus. Now they saw the outcome, and began to have new insight and faith in Jesus, having received this glimpse of his glory.

"You see," Jesus said quietly to his followers, "G-d saves the best for last, and when the bridegroom is in your midst, it is right for everyone to celebrate. Everyone." This was the first of Jesus' miracles that revealed something important about his identity, as witnessed by both his disciples and his mother. His brothers and sisters who were also present, including James, had not seen what transpired, although they had certainly enjoyed the final round of toasts along with everyone else.

When the wedding was over, Jesus invited his family members to come with him back to Kefer Nahum for a few days, and see where he had established the base for his ministry. They agreed. He wanted them to know he was in a good place, and was certainly not idly avoiding family responsibilities, but doing G-d's work.

11

Shabbat Controversy

IT WAS FRIDAY and already well past noon, so the travelers walked at a swift pace to reach Kefer Nahum in time for the Shabbat service in the village synagogue. Built within a hundred yards of the sea, this synagogue of stone had served the community well as both a place of worship and a community center for all sorts of purposes, including the study of Torah. Jesus, his brothers, sisters, and mother, as well as the seven disciples, arrived at the fishing village late in the afternoon, just in time to wash at the house of Simon's mother-in-law and head straight to the synagogue.

As they approached, they heard the sound of singing. But when Jesus entered the place, the people saw him and quickly fell into silence, except for the whispers. "There he is. The healer. He's back." Jesus walked into the portico of the synagogue and noticed an older man with a withered hand standing just inside the doorway, hoping to go unnoticed by the congregation. Jesus looked at the man, saw his need, and felt keenly aware that those gathered had turned around to see what he would do.

Would he heal on Shabbat? The rules about work on Shabbat were complex, but in essence they boiled down to the notion that nothing except an absolute emergency should be undertaken on Shabbat. Everything else could wait until after sundown on Saturday.

Jesus walked into the middle of the synagogue and beckoned to the man, "Come forward." He scanned the congregation before asking, "Is it lawful to do good or to do harm on Shabbat? To save life or to kill?" No one responded. The room was deathly quiet, as if all were holding their breath, waiting to see what would happen. Jesus looked around again, but this time in anger, grieved by the hardness of their hearts. Then he said to the man, "Stretch out your hand."

Visibly shaking from the strain of being the center of attention, yet desperate for the healing that would return his ability to work, the old man stretched out his hand. And suddenly, quite visibly, his hand was restored. This instantly shattered the silence, as everyone began speaking at once. Some of the Pharisees and Herodians, clearly incensed, stood and left, casting murderous glances at Jesus as they filed out. What further evidence did they need that this teacher was not a godly man, as the villagers had claimed? Clearly he did not respect Shabbat law. The healing could have waited a few hours. After all, the man had been waiting for most of his life. What difference would a few hours more have made? But to Jesus, it was the perfect time to give the man "restoration" from what ailed him, to enter the rest of Shabbat. Wasn't that the original purpose of Shabbat—to celebrate shalom, the wholeness and goodness of G-d's creation?

The synagogue president eventually restored order, and the Shabbat service was concluded. Afterward, Jesus' brother James came to him, almost shaking with fury. "Was that wise? Couldn't it have waited? Did you have to do it so publicly? Now you've alienated the local authorities. It's bad enough that your family has to live with the shame of your abandoning us, but now . . . now the word 'scandal' will be attached to our name! Why did you have to do that here and now?"

Jesus' response was direct and pointed. "People weren't created for Shabbat, to observe it, to serve it. Rather, Shabbat was set up for the good of people! And furthermore, the Son of Man is Lord over Shabbat. G-d's dominion, his divine saving activity, is breaking into our world, saving and healing people, and new occasions teach new duties, new ways of viewing and doing things."

He laid a hand gently on James' arm. "And my brother, the heart of the Law is compassion and mercy. How could I refuse to heal him when I have the ability to do so?"

James pulled his arm away, simply appalled at this rebuttal. He was a very traditional Jew, observant of the Law, and to him Jesus' action seemed at best arrogant, and at worst a breaking of the Law of Moses. His brothers were puzzled as well. How could Jesus do miracles, if not by G-d's power? But would G-d sanction such irregularity on Shabbat?

They left the synagogue and began walking back to the home of Simon's mother-in-law, Naomi. They passed a small wheat field and several of the disciples were so hungry, they began plucking some of the ripe grain, rubbing the husks off between their palms before eating it.

Two Pharisees who were following the group at a short distance called out to Jesus. "Why are your followers doing what is not lawful on Shabbat?"

Jesus turned to them. "Haven't you ever read what David did when he was in need, when he and those with him were hungry?

During the time when Abiathar was high priest, David went into G-d's house and ate the bread of the presence, which only the priests were allowed to eat. He also gave bread to those who were with him."

Then Jesus told them, "Shabbat was created for humans; humans weren't created for Shabbat. This is why the Son of Man is Lord, even over Shabbat and its rules."

"Who is this Son of Man?" asked one of the Pharisees. "And is he as great or important as King David?" Jesus did not answer the man, preferring instead to leave them to ponder his words.

The family and disciples arrived at the courtyard of Naomi's house and they entered, leaving the Pharisees to stare at Jesus' back as he walked inside. His sisters cast uneasy looks back to where the Pharisees had turned on their heels and stormed off. Jesus' family was clearly uneasy with all that had transpired on this Shabbat. Even Mary was puzzled and did not know what to think. But unlike James, who was ready to condemn Jesus, she stored these things up in her heart and meditated on their meaning.

Jesus, for his part, saw nothing wrong with anything that had happened. He seemed to enjoy the simple evening meal and conversation around the table with Simon's family and the disciples. But his family, while they ate readily enough, was strangely silent and could not be coaxed into talking. That is, all except Mary, who talked at length about the family wedding and the miracle of new wine that had happened in Qana. Clearly, she was trying to put a good face on things for Jesus' sake.

At first light, James insisted to Mary that they return to Netzerit. He was not comfortable staying any longer in Kefer Nahum with the disciples and Simon's family, and made the excuse that the brothers would need to be back at work early

Sunday morning. He feared the word would soon spread that Jesus was a Shabbat-breaker, and that his disciples were lax in their observance of the day as well. James was sure that no good could come of this, as were others among Jesus' brothers, and he did not want the rest of the family to be tarred with the same brush. He took his responsibility to maintain the honor of his family seriously, even if his older brother apparently did not. It didn't take a prophet to see that storm clouds were beginning to hang on the horizon. James had no intention of allowing the family to get caught up in the trouble he feared was coming—which, he believed, would be soon.

12

A Warm Welcome

JESUS REALIZED IT would be wise for him to get away from Kefer Nahum for a while. So he told his disciples they should remain and work there for a few days before celebrating Rosh Hashanah, the beginning of a new year, and he would return after the festival. He told them that he would be celebrating in Yerushalayim, and staying with friends nearby.

He decided to take a less travelled road on this occasion, going through Samaria and down into Judaea. There would be less of a chance of being recognized if he went this way, because most pious Jews never went through Samaria. They saw it as an unclean land full of unclean persons, so they preferred to take the road heading south on the other side of the Jordan down to Jericho, and then cross the Jordan to enter Judaea. Jesus took his time on the seventy-mile journey, stopping along the way near Sychar and Mount Gerizim, then again in the northern part of Judaea, and finally reaching the small town of Bet Anya, just beyond the Mount of Olives.

Bet Anya was the home of Lazarus and his two sisters. Jesus had promised Lazarus that he would come for a visit, and when

71

he knocked on their door that morning in the middle of the week and asked if he could enter, there was an immediate flurry of activity. Martha, the older of the two sisters, greeted him at the door and said, "Of course, you must come in, Master. Lazarus has spoken often of you, but we were unsure when you might be coming. He is away today on business, but I anticipate his return this evening."

Mary, the younger sister, removed Jesus' sandals and washed his feet because he had come into the house off the dusty roads. She gave him a small bowl and a cloth to wash his hands and face. Then, in another gracious act of hospitality, she anointed his head with oil to keep his scalp from cracking in the heat.

Martha was in her late twenties, a tall, robust—almost muscular—"take charge" type. Mary was much shorter, small-framed, quiet, shy, and contemplative, more serious in her piety and devotion to Torah than her sister. Jesus sat down in the front room where Mary was sitting and began to have a conversation with her, while Martha bustled about in the cooking area of the small mud-brick house preparing a meal for them to share together.

"So Mary, tell me what Lazarus said to you about John the Baptizer, and what has been going on at the Jordan."

"Like many others," Mary replied, "for some time we have been looking for the restoration of Israel, of G-d's people, and the land itself. Our life under Rome is becoming worse every day. Of course, here in Judaea, we are now ruled by a procurator, Pontius Pilate. I'm sure you are aware that he has no great affection for our people, and shows little respect for our religion and our customs. There have been several incidents since he arrived a year ago, none of them good. The most horrific one happened only recently. Pilate got angry with some pilgrims from Galilee, and had them executed, their own blood mingling with that of their sacrifices! Just shocking, horrible. The earlier incidents produced a great enough furor here that a delegation was sent to Rome about Pilate's flagrant violations of our customs, and his lack of respect for us as a people."

She leaned forward conspiratorially. "Rumor has it that he has been put on notice by Emperor Tiberius that he needs to be more cooperative with our religious leaders, and less vicious, less venal in his actions toward us. Any more slip-ups, and no doubt the emperor will no longer call him 'friend of Caesar.' He will call him, 'troublemaker.'"

"That is terrible. Most troubling," said Jesus. "But, as Lazarus has no doubt told you, John is saying that G-d will soon intervene in judgment on the corruption in the land: both Jewish corruption—since judgment begins with the household of G-d—as well as what the pagans have brought. I do not disagree with John, but I am here to tell you a slightly different story, a story about the good news of G-d's saving activity already breaking into our midst through what G-d has sent me, and my disciples, to do."

While Mary sat quietly, listening intently to him, Jesus could hear Martha muttering to herself in the other room. Suddenly she stepped out of the cooking area and said to Jesus, "Master, do you not care that my sister has left me to do all the work myself, while she sits at your feet and just soaks up your marvelous teaching? Tell her to come help me!"

As Mary rose in response to these words, Jesus turned to the older sister and said, "Martha, Martha, you are worried about and distracted by many things. But just now there is need of only one thing, and Mary has chosen the better dish, the better food, and it will not be taken away from her."

The usually very vocal Martha was, at first, left speechless by this response. Then she said, almost incredulously, "You mean, you think that studying the work and word of G-d is the main thing, the top priority not only for men, but for women as well? And that even we have a right to put that first in our lives?"

"That's exactly what I'm saying," said Jesus, "and this is especially so since G-d's final, divine, saving activity is now breaking into our lives. We all need to understand and receive, and believe in it—women and children and slaves included—not just free Jewish men."

The conversation went on for a while as Martha, and occasionally Mary, asked questions. The afternoon had begun to wane when they heard a knock at the door, and Lazarus entered without waiting for anyone to welcome him home. As soon as he spotted their guest, a huge grin spread across his face. Jesus rose from his seat, and Lazarus, extremely pleased to see him, gave him a hug and a kiss of greeting on the cheek.

"There is great excitement in Judaea about what has been happening," Lazarus told him. "John's message and baptisms have excited many, and so have you! Everyone's talking about the miracles that you are said to have performed. Are the stories true?"

"I'm not sure about *all* the stories you've heard," Jesus responded. "But yes, I have performed both healings and exorcisms. And there has been no little controversy about them, not least because I have chosen to do some of these things on Shabbat."

"On Shabbat? Really?" asked Lazarus. "Was it some kind of emergency?"

"All things are urgent now that the time is fulfilled and the dominion of G-d is at hand," Jesus replied. "We have reached the end of days. Everything has changed and the true time of Jubilee now begins with release of the captives. The spiritually and the socially bound are freed, good news is preached to the poor, and healing is brought to the lame."

Lazarus took all of this in, and said, "Those who are favorably impressed by you are saying that you are like other northern prophets, Elijah, or Elisha. But your public teaching seems to be like one of the sages or seers of old—all those parables, riddles, and aphorisms about G-d's dominion." He shook his head. "I must confess I do not understand all of this. One thing that *is* clear to me is that you have some excited sympathizers here in Bet Anya, not least our family, and you have piqued the curiosity of at least one important Jewish elder, a teacher and member of the Sanhedrin, a man named Nicodemus. Now that you are here, I will take the liberty to arrange a time of meeting with him, perhaps as early as tonight, if you are not too tired.

"Of course," Lazarus continued, "you also have your detractors, both for healing on Shabbat and for the exorcisms. Some are even whispering that you must be in league with the Adversary to have such power and authority over unclean spirits. Some of the Pharisees seem especially concerned about this sort of activity on your part. And is it really true that you have dined with sinners— the unclean—sharing table fellowship with tax collectors and the notoriously immoral?"

Jesus nodded. "Yes, all these things are true." His voice became firm. "For have I not come to call the sinners especially, and to heal the sick? I was sent to the lost sheep of Israel, but G-d's saving activity is for everyone else as well."

"Well, I suggest you explain some of these things to Nicodemus," replied Lazarus. "It would be good to have a Pharisee who could speak up for you." He smiled, and gestured toward the low table, set for supper. "But only after we eat!"

Lazarus called out, "Martha, what have you prepared for dinner tonight?"

"I thought we'd never get around to something practical like that," said Martha with some exasperation. She emerged from the kitchen, wiping her hands on her apron. "We have some soup to start with, and then there will be some fresh vegetables and olives, of course, and some leavened bread with a nice relish for dipping. We will drink some of the new wine, and we will finish with some really lovely dates, figs, and nuts."

Jesus clapped his hands together. "Wonderful! And then after dinner I will have that chat with Nicodemus, as you suggest." Mary helped Martha to bring out the food, and after everyone sat down, Lazarus asked Jesus to say the blessing over the meal. He did so, lifting the bread and reciting the *hamotzi* prayer: "Blessed are you O G-d, King of the Universe, who brings forth bread from the earth." He then broke the bread and passed it to Mary.

The meal time passed quickly, with much good conversation amid an air of conviviality. Jesus already loved this family and saw that this home, like the home of Simon's mother-in-law in Kefer Nahum, could serve as a base of operations when he was in Judaea. But he also realized that his approach in Judaea would need to be different than in Galilee, both in his teaching and his healing.

Indeed, Judaea was a different place, particularly since it had become a Roman province not long after the death of

Herod the Great, when Jesus was still quite young. There was a reason John the Baptizer did not come directly into Judaea to minister, even though he had relatives there. In many ways, it was a dangerous place for itinerant prophets, and unauthorized teachers and healers. Here, and especially in Yerushalayim, suspected prophetic and messianic figures were watched most carefully, and were in danger of falling afoul of the law—not just Jewish law, but Roman law.

Unlike Galilee, there were many priests and Levites in Judaea, and their scribes—experts in the Law of Moses—were also quite numerous. A thousand eyes examined all forms of ministry in and around the capital city, and those eyes were always looking for something wrong. They kept a very close watch on any religious teacher, preacher, or healer who came from beyond the borders of Judaea, beyond their circle of control. Nevertheless, Jesus felt he could talk in confidence with this family, without fear.

He also had considerable affection for them, especially in light of the trauma they had lived through. Simon, their father, had died of a dreaded skin disease, leprosy. Not only had it left its physical mark on Simon and led to his death, it had also left a spiritual mark and stigma on the family. Even though Lazarus, Martha, and Mary were all free of the disease, and scrupulous in their attention to issues of hygiene and ritual purity, the memory of what had happened lingered in Bet Anya. And so none of Simon's children had been able to marry; their overtures to others were rebuffed for fear that the disease would spread beyond their household. Such was the fear of leprosy. But Jesus felt right at home with these people, and relished the warm welcome that both his presence and his message had received. Perhaps because they, of all people, needed the promise of the better day he proclaimed in word and deed—a day when all uncleanness and impurity would be completely banished.

It was decided that the meeting with Nicodemus would take place in their home. But given the Pharisee's high social standing in town, they also felt the conversation should be a private one where the two men could speak freely. So the three siblings stepped out for a while, leaving Jesus alone and waiting for Nicodemus to come.

13

Nicodemus

THE MOON HAD risen quite high in the night sky when Nicodemus arrived at the house. He took one last look to the left and right before knocking, and entered quickly. It was best that his fellow Pharisees and members of the Sanhedrin did not know about this visit, lest tongues start wagging and his position in those circles become compromised.

Mary and Martha returned shortly after this, and when they saw the two men, they quietly made their way through to the sleeping area. Lazarus chose to stay away a little longer, to give Jesus some privacy and space.

Jesus offered his guest some wine. Nicodemus was a man in his fifties with a long, white beard. His robe looked expensive and he wore a head covering and a black-and-white prayer shawl, looking every inch the Pharisaic teacher. As such, Nicodemus began the conversation with characteristic directness.

"Master, we know you are a teacher who has come from G-d, for no one could perform the miraculous signs you are doing if G-d was not with him."

Jesus nodded in response to this, and said, "Amen, amen, I say to you, no one can see the dominion of G-d unless he is born again, born from above."

"How can a man be born when he is old?" Nicodemus asked. "Surely he cannot enter a second time into his mother's womb to be born again!"

"Amen, amen, I tell you, no one can enter the dominion of G-d unless he is born out of water and the Spirit. Flesh gives birth to flesh, but the Spirit gives birth to spirit. You should not be surprised at my saying, 'You must be born again.' The wind blows wherever it pleases. You hear its sound, but you cannot tell where it comes from or where it is going. So it is with everyone born of the Spirit."

"How can this be?" Nicodemus persisted.

"You are one of Israel's most respected teachers, and do you not understand these things? Amen, amen, I tell you, we speak of what we know, and we testify to what we have seen, but still people like you do not accept our testimony. I have spoken to you of earthly things and you do not believe; how then will you believe if I speak of heavenly things? No one has ever gone into heaven, except the One who came from heaven, the Son of Man. Just as Moses lifted up the snake in the desert, so the Son of Man must be lifted up, that everyone who believes in him may have eternal life."

Nicodemus still seemed confused as Jesus continued. "For G-d so loved the world that he gave his only Son, so that everyone who believes in him will not perish but will have everlasting life. G-d did not send his Son into the world to judge the world, but that the world might be saved through him. Whoever believes in him is not judged; whoever does not believe in him is already judged, because they do not believe in the name of G-d's only Son."

Nicodemus held Jesus' gaze as he lifted the cup of wine to his lips. Jesus leaned forward, speaking earnestly. "This is the basis for judgment: the light came into the world, but people loved darkness more than the light, for their actions are evil. All who do wicked things hate the light, and don't come to the light for fear that their actions will be exposed to the light. Whoever practices the truth comes to the light, so that it can be seen that their actions were done in G-d."

Nicodemus felt the sting in Jesus' words, looking a bit self-conscious because of his own visit under cover of darkness. But perhaps the most astounding and offensive part, to him, was the radical notion that even a pious old Jewish man like himself needed to be born again, to be born from above, to be born of G-d. Had he not been born a son of Abraham? What did it mean to be born again?

Yet, Nicodemus saw how intent Jesus was to make this point clear. He recognized that just as John was calling all to repentance, Jesus was also calling both the high and the low, both the pious and impious, both the sinner and the holy man to repentance—to be changed. Radically changed.

It was to his credit that Nicodemus did not immediately reject or object to Jesus' earnest appeal. Instead, he simply wondered, perhaps even worried how these things could be true. And if they were, how would his fellow Jewish leaders take the news that G-d wanted them to repent and start over again on their spiritual journey? Looking into Jesus' eyes, he chuckled at the thought of what their reaction would be. He also found it interesting, if not strange, that Jesus pronounced the "Amen" to his own teachings in advance of enunciating what they were. It was as if he could verify the truth of his own words, and did not need outside witnesses to do so. But what was the source of his authority?

The conversation came to an end. Nicodemus rose to leave, saying to Jesus, "Until another time. *Shalom aleichem.*"

"*Aleichem shalom,*" Jesus responded with a smile. Having returned the parting blessing of peace, he briefly embraced a somewhat surprised Nicodemus, then saw him to the door. The Pharisee walked away, passed Lazarus returning home, and offered a wry smile along with his blessing of peace.

Lazarus entered his home and immediately asked Jesus, "So how did that go? Did he receive your radical message of the dominion of G-d with gladness?"

"Perhaps not immediately with gladness, but I believe he is ruminating on it. I imagine his scholarly mind has been teased into active thought, so it is a beginning. A small beginning in the right direction, G-d be praised. And now I must get some rest, as tomorrow I plan to walk to the Pool of Siloam and visit those who come there seeking healing."

Lazarus grimaced. "Well, that will certainly attract some attention, but then I guess you can hardly avoid attention any longer."

"Indeed," replied Jesus. "Besides, the night is coming when I will no longer be able to work, so I must make the most of the time while it is still day." With those words, he departed to the small guest room.

Now, what does that mean? wondered Lazarus.

14

Who Is My Neighbor?

ONE OF THE things Jesus had reflected on during his stay in Bet Anya was the different mission and ministry strategies that would be required in Judaea to proclaim the good news about the in-breaking dominion of G-d. Short, pithy wisdom sayings and parables were appropriate in the Galilee, but this was unlikely to be effective here in Judaea, nor as a main approach to his teaching in Yerushalayim. He needed to be more direct, even if he chose to use wisdom speech to convey his message.

Jesus also recognized that, while he would perform miracles in and around Yerushalayim even on Shabbat if the need arose, it may be wise to avoid doing exorcisms there. The atmosphere in and around Yerushalayim was already too highly charged due to the presence of the brutal procurator, Pilate, and exorcisms might produce panic if not hysteria. And it would surely embolden the *kana'im*, whom Jesus saw no need to encourage.

The *kana'im*—those "zealous on behalf of G-d," or "Zealots," from the Greek word—had demonized the Roman rulers as the incarnation of evil in their midst. Thus, exorcisms in the very region where they most wanted a revolt could be seen as an implicit approval from Jesus, if not a call to take violent action. The thinking went that if the devil was being overthrown spiritually by exorcisms, and those held captive by demons were being liberated, then surely it was time to overthrow the surrogates of Satan—Pilate and his minions—and liberate the politically oppressed.

Knowing this, Jesus was glad that he had recruited a couple of traveling disciples who were involved at one time or another with the Zealots. One of these was a man named Simon, and the other, a Judaean named Judas. Jesus thought it wise for his closest disciples to form a cross section of Jewish society, including representatives of people considered to be on the margins of civilized, pious society: tax collectors, sinners, and yes, Zealots. They would all be a part of G-d's coming dominion.

Judas had, in fact, belonged to an extreme element within the Zealots, the so-called *sicarii* or "dagger men," those who killed fellow Jews who they saw collaborating with the Romans. This is where Judas' nickname—Iscariot—had come from. Judas also had organizational skills, and he had raised and managed money for the Zealots. Jesus knew it was a risk to recruit such a person into his inner circle, especially given that the sicarii had often targeted tax collectors like Matthew. But the good news of non-violent liberation could hardly have a better testimony than from a once violent man who had been changed, transformed by word of the in-breaking dominion of G-d.

These were Jesus' thoughts as he walked down the Mount of Olives into the Kidron Valley and around to the Sheep Gate on the northwestern side of the city of Yerushalayim. From there a pool called Bet Zatha or Bet Hesda—"house of mercy"—came into view. It was one of the many pools and cisterns around Yerushalayim, some of them fed by springs, where water was allowed to collect both within and outside—but always near—the city walls. Such places were especially in demand during the summer months, since rainfall was rare in Yerushalayim.

This particular pool had five porticoes. In these lay a multitude of those who were sick, blind, lame, or had withered limbs. Many believed that the waters of the pool were stirred up by an angel from time to time, and if you were the first person into the water, you would be healed of what ailed you. A man lay there who had been ill for thirty-eight years. When Jesus saw him, and knew that he had suffered for such a long time in that condition, he said to him, "Do you want to get well?"

"Sir," the sick man responded, "I don't have anyone who can put me in the water when it is stirred up. When I'm trying to get to it, someone else goes in ahead of me."

"Stop making excuses. Get up! Pick up your mat and walk." Immediately, the man was well, and did as Jesus told him.

As it happened, this was on Shabbat. Some of the Jewish authorities saw the man who had been healed carrying his mat, and they confronted him. "It's Shabbat," they said. "You aren't allowed to carry your mat."

He answered, "The man who made me well said to me, 'Pick up your mat and walk.'"

"Who is this man?" they demanded. But the man who had been cured didn't know who it was, because Jesus had slipped away from the crowd at the pool.

Later Jesus found the healed man in the temple and said, "See! You have been made well. Don't sin anymore, in case something worse happens to you." The man then went and proclaimed to the Jewish authorities that Jesus was the one who had made him well. Jesus did not want credit for the healing, nor did he wish to use it to prove to anyone who he was; he had simply wanted the man to be cured. But the Jewish authorities began harassing him, because he had done the healing on Shabbat.

Jesus responded to their criticism, saying, "My Father is still working, and I am working too." This was one of the reasons some of the Jewish authorities began to make plans to deal with Jesus, should he stay in Yerushalayim. But Jesus, knowing what was in their hearts and minds, slipped out of town and headed back to Galilee, this time along the Jericho road.

✝ ✝ ✝

The winding road from Yerushalayim to Jericho, geographically the lowest city on earth, drops several thousand feet in the span of only twenty miles, making the descent a challenge in places. Jesus found himself traveling with some priests and Levites, as well as a few of their experts in the Mosaic Law. Many such men commuted from Jericho to Yerushalayim and back again, because they could not afford to live on Mount Zion where Caiaphas and other well-to-do priests, Levites, and scribes lived.

One of the experts in the Law, a young man with a keen mind for legal distinctions and problems, struck up a conversation with Jesus on a subject that was frequently debated: what the term "neighbor" in the Mosaic Law actually meant. He particularly wanted clarity on who did *not* count as his neighbor, a matter about which he had some strong ideas.

"Teacher," the young man said to Jesus, "what must I do to inherit everlasting life?"

"What is written in the Law?" Jesus replied. "How do you read it?"

"'Love the Lord your G-d with all your heart and with all your soul and with all your strength and with all your mind.' And, 'Love your neighbor as yourself.'"

"You have answered correctly. Do this and you will live."

But the lawyer wanted to justify himself, so he asked Jesus, "But who is my neighbor?"

Jesus looked intently into the young man's eyes for a few moments, and then gestured back toward Yerushalayim. "A man went down from Yerushalayim to Jericho," he began. "The man encountered thieves, who stripped him naked, beat him up, and left him near death." Jesus pointed with his head toward the men in costly robes who were walking ahead of them.

"Now it just so happened that a priest was also going down the same road. When he saw the injured man, he crossed over to the other side of the road and went on his way. Likewise, a Levite came by that spot, saw the injured man, and crossed over to the other side of the road and went on his way."

Jesus stopped, and took the arm of the young scribe. "A Samaritan, who was on a journey, came upon the injured man, and was moved with compassion. The Samaritan bandaged the man's wounds, tending them with oil and wine. Then he placed the man on his own donkey, took him to an inn, and took care of him. The next day, he took two full days' worth of wages and gave them to the innkeeper. He said, 'Take care of him, and when I return, I will pay you back for any additional costs.'"

Jesus looked intently into the young man's face before saying, "What do you think? Which one of these three was a neighbor to the man who encountered the thieves?"

The expert in the law, clearly displeased by the ending of the story, pulled his arm away from Jesus' grip. As he did so, he became aware that his fellow scribes had stopped and were regarding him with keen interest. He had meant to test Jesus with his question, but somehow Jesus had reversed the situation. The scribal class looked down on Samaritans for their lack of proper Jewish piety. But Jesus had backed him into a corner with this story, and so, gritting his teeth and grimacing, he reluctantly answered, "I suppose it was the one who had mercy on him."

Jesus held his gaze for a moment before saying, "Go and do likewise."

This was too much for the young man. "Go and be like a Samaritan? But there are no good Samaritans! They are the enemies of good and pious men!" he said, with some heat.

"But what if your enemy is also your neighbor?" said Jesus with a wry smile. The scribe's face flushed. Jesus started to move on, then turned sharply. "Instead of asking, 'Who is worthy of being my neighbor?' perhaps you could ask yourself, 'How can I be a neighbor to whoever is in need of help?' For are not all made in the image of G-d, and worthy of our care?" With this Jesus turned and walked swiftly away, gaining on and then passing the priests and Levites, who scowled at his back. He left the young man and his colleagues muttering darkly about this scandalous teaching.

When Jesus reached Jericho, he immediately crossed the Jordan and headed north once more on the main road. As he walked, he thought back to the expressions on the faces around him as he had told the story and the disapproval he had seen writ large there. He would need to keep moving around if he was to avoid trouble, or else—and at this thought he shook his head and sighed deeply—change his message and methods.

His jaw tightened, and he lifted his head. He would not do that, for he had been charged by G-d, his Abba, to tell one and all of the final saving activity of G-d; to proclaim that G-d's dominion had come, and was infiltrating the hearts and minds and homes of all who heard the good news.

15

Healing in Kefer Nahum

MUCH HAD HAPPENED since Jesus had left Kefer Nahum. The ministries of John and Jesus were the talk of Galilee. Many people wondered why the two men were so different. Others thought they might be working together, because they were kin. When Jesus reached the house of Simon's mother-in-law, there was great joy—but also some anxiety—at seeing him again. He knew the crowds would return soon, those desperate for healing and help, but for now he wanted to concentrate on forming his disciples into an organized band with leadership. Jesus had decided on Simon, James, and John to be the inner circle for his Galilean ministry.

He would choose twelve men—from both Galilee and Judaea and from all walks of life—but not, as some might think, to be the nucleus of a *new* Israel. They would, instead, be his co-laborers in freeing the twelve tribes, helping to find and save "the lost sheep" of Israel. Jesus would teach them, train them, empower them, and send them out to be his arms and legs all across Galilee, extending his ministry in all directions.

But that was not all. When he returned to Kefer Nahum, Jesus was approached by one of the first persons he had ever healed or helped in Galilee, Miryam of Migdal. She asked if she and some other women could also become learners and be his disciples. To her great surprise, Jesus immediately said, "Yes." He became the first Jewish teacher, sage, or prophet in that age to have women followers who were not related to him. This caused yet more scandal in conservative Jewish circles. Exactly who did this upstart teacher from Netzerit think he was?

Calling together the Twelve, Jesus led them up to the cliffs of Arbel, and stood with them on top of this place from which one could see in all directions. Jesus said to them, "Behold the Galilee. I am appointing you to be my *shalihim*, my agents, particularly in Galilee. I will be sending you out two by two, since, according to the Law of Moses, the testimony of two witnesses is needed to verify the truth of anything. Your task will be to do the very same things you have seen me do: proclaim the good news of the in-breaking dominion of G-d, heal the sick, and cast out demons. To that end, today I am authorizing and empowering you for this ministry."

Having said this, Jesus laid hands on each of the Twelve, to commission them one after the other, beginning with Simon. Then came the Zebedees, to whom he gave the nickname Boanerges ("Sons of Thunder"), then on to Andrew (Simon's brother), and Philip, Bartholomew, and Matthew—the tax collector and scribe of the group. Then it was Thomas' turn, followed by James (son of Alphaeus), and Thaddaeus (whose

Hebrew name was Nathan'el). Last were the two Judaeans, Simon the Zealot or "Qanaean," as he was also known, and Judas Iscariot.

When Jesus went back down with the Twelve into the village, they found two people anxiously waiting for him. The first was a messenger from his cousin John, with some terrible news. John had been taken captive by that old fox, Herod Antipas, and sent to the prison called Machereus on the other side of the Jordan. Jesus thanked the messenger and asked him to relay a word of peace to John, and to continue to give him updates about John's welfare. As the messenger left, Jesus shook his head. This did not bode well. It meant that Herod was even prepared to act against a prophet who was popular with the people of both Judaea and Galilee. What might he do about Jesus himself, if put under pressure from the scribes and Pharisees?

This also meant that the time had come for Jesus to return to Netzerit, to present his manifesto, his first major sermon explaining the character of his ministry. He was under no illusion that this would be received with much joy or gladness in his hometown. Still, it needed to be done there, since he was known to all as Jesus from Netzerit. It was also appropriate because this was the town where the descendants of David lived in Galilee. The image of his cousin in chains suddenly came to his mind. He turned to the Twelve and said, "Of all men born of women, John is the greatest. But even the least in the dominion of G-d is greater than he. He is the last of the great prophets of old, and the Law and the prophets have been until and including John."

One of the Twelve interrupted and said, "Some say John is the Elijah figure who was foretold by the prophet Malachi—the one coming before the great and terrible day of G-d's judgment."

Jesus responded, "To be sure, Elijah comes and will restore all things. But I tell you, Elijah has already come, and they did not recognize him, but have done to him everything they wished. In the same way, the Son of Man is going to suffer at their hands." The disciples had no response to this, as they did not understand what Jesus meant. In any case, there was no time to ponder it, as someone else was waiting anxiously to speak to Jesus at the edge of Kefer Nahum.

Jairus, the leader of the synagogue, frantically pleaded for Jesus to come with him. His twelve-year-old daughter was very ill, perhaps even dying. Jairus fell at Jesus' feet, an act of humiliating deference that caused a small stir among those looking on. He begged Jesus to come quickly to his house and lay hands on his little girl. Jesus agreed to do this, and dismissed all the Twelve except Simon, James, and John, who he told to come with him as witnesses. They then left for the house, knowing it would be difficult to get in because a huge crowd had accompanied Jairus, a well-respected and beloved elder of the town.

The crowd followed them, pressing in on Jesus from all sides. A woman was there who had been bleeding for twelve years. She had suffered a great deal under the care of many doctors and had spent all her money on treatments, yet her condition only worsened. When she heard Jesus was there, she came up behind him in the crowd and touched his cloak, thinking, *If I can just touch the fringes of his garment, I will be healed.* Immediately, her bleeding stopped, and she felt in her body that she was freed from her suffering.

But at once Jesus realized that power had gone out from him. He turned around in the crowd, scanning the faces, and asked, "Who touched my clothes?"

"You see the people crowding against you," said his disciples incredulously, "and yet you can ask, 'Who touched me?'" But Jesus kept looking around to see who had done it. Then the woman, knowing what had happened to her, came and fell at his feet and, trembling with fear, told him the whole truth.

Jesus said to her, "Daughter, it is your faith that has healed you, not some magic in my garments. Go in peace and be freed from your suffering."

While Jesus was still speaking, some men came from the house of Jairus. Their grief-stricken faces told Jairus their message before they spoke. "Your daughter is dead," they said. "No need to bother the teacher anymore. There's nothing he can do now."

Ignoring the men, Jesus spoke to Jairus. "Look at me. Don't be afraid; just believe." *Believe like that woman believed*, Jesus thought.

When they reached the home, Jesus didn't let anyone follow him inside except Simon, James, John, and Jairus. They walked to the outer courtyard and Jesus saw the commotion, people crying loudly. He went in and said to them, "Why all this commotion and wailing? The child is not dead, but asleep." But those from the town who were professional mourners, one who played a wind instrument and a woman who was paid to wail on behalf of the family, laughed at Jesus. *Not dead? Then why had they been summoned?* It was normal to have a full week of mourning after a death, and they had wasted no time in beginning the process.

Much to their chagrin, Jesus put these people out of the house. He took Jairus, the child's mother, and the disciples who were with him, and went in to where the child lay. The girl was very still, not breathing. The pallor of death had settled on her small face. Jairus trembled at Jesus' side. Jesus reached down and gently took her by the hand. He spoke in a soft voice, in Aramaic, saying, "*Talitha koum!*" which means, "Little girl, I say to you, get up!" Immediately, the girl stood up and walked around. Both the family and the three disciples were completely astonished and struck dumb. He gave strict orders for them to continue their silence about the matter, not letting anyone know what had happened.

He looked at the young girl and told them to give her something to eat. Her mother rushed to the kitchen to find something. Jairus swept his daughter up into his arms, looking at Jesus through tear-filled eyes. Jesus smiled at him, then led his disciples out of the room and through the crowded courtyard.

As they left Jairus' house, he told the three, "We must get to work, especially now that John's ministry has been cut short. The first step is to go to Netzerit, this very afternoon, as Shabbat is coming. I need to address the people of my hometown, my family, as they will have heard many things about my ministry in the last weeks—some of them true, some of them false."

As Jesus spoke, Simon could tell from the expression on his face that he did not relish the prospect of returning home. He looked more like a man bracing himself for something unpleasant, and Simon would soon understand why.

16

A Rough Homecoming

ON THIS OCCASION, Jesus led his disciples on a slightly different path through the hills to Netzerit. They entered the little village of Nain, just a few miles from Jesus' hometown. A considerable crowd now accompanied Jesus everywhere he went, begging for healing and help.

As they approached the town gate, the body of a dead man was being carried out, the only son of his widowed mother. A large procession of townspeople followed behind. When Jesus saw the woman, his heart went out to her. Jesus knew that because this widow had lost her only son, she could then lose her home and property to one of her husband's male relatives. Thus the situation had the potential for twofold tragedy: not only had she lost a child, but her own future might well depend on the good will of a distant relation—a scenario that Jesus knew did not always end well for the widow.

He approached her and said, "Do not weep." The widow turned toward the stranger, a look of bewilderment mixing with the tears of grief. Jesus gently laid his hand on her arm, and then strode forward.

He reached out and touched the bier, and a collective gasp escaped from the crowd because he made himself ritually unclean by doing so. Those carrying it stood still. Jesus said, "Young man, I say to you, rise up!" And the dead man sat up and began to talk! Jesus then took him by the hand and gave him back to his mother.

Both the disciples and the crowd were filled with awe, and they praised G-d together. "A great prophet has appeared among us," they said. "G-d has come to help his people!" This news about Jesus spread as far as Judaea, as well as the surrounding countryside in Galilee. Unlike the raising of Jairus' daughter, this action was public, and Jesus realized he would soon have such a reputation that there would be no place to run and hide.

They continued on their journey from Nain to Netzerit, and arrived just as the sun began to set. Jesus stopped first at his family's home, and Mary came out to greet him. Giving her a warm embrace, he said to her, "Tell the synagogue leader I am here and would like to address the townspeople."

Mary leaned away from Jesus, examining his face. She was silent for a moment and then said, "Are you sure about this? There is so much gossip about you in this town, some of it very negative. Speaking in the synagogue may appear . . . provocative."

Jesus smiled, tracing the lines of concern in his mother's face with his fingertips. "Nevertheless," he said, "I need to announce publicly what I am doing, which is a fulfillment of the sacred writings. And here is certainly the right place to start that work. Send someone over to the ruler's house and tell him I am on my way."

His face fell a little. "Did you hear that Antipas has taken John prisoner?"

"Yes, the news reached us just yesterday. And it only added to my worries about you. Don't you see that you're putting yourself in danger if you keep following this path you're on? And what's this that Joses just ran into the house to tell me? You raised a boy from the dead just down the road in Nain? You touched his corpse first?"

Jesus nodded. Mary's eyes grew wide, before saying, "Well *that* will certainly draw a crowd this evening, and a lot of unwelcome attention, I assure you! Your brother James says that you're beginning to act like a mad man—defying the authorities, and violating our customs about things clean and unclean." She looked over his shoulder to the street, where the disciples waited for Jesus to rejoin them. "And who are those men out there? I recognize the fishermen from Kefer Nahum, but who are the others? Is it true you have even recruited some Zealots? What are you thinking? Are you deliberately provoking Herod? His actions this week show us he believes your cousin is politically dangerous. And John hasn't raised people from the dead!"

Jesus listened to these worries, and then said, "Mother, Mother. It is all in G-d's plan and will for me, as you surely know. I must follow the script laid out in the Scriptures." He smiled. "Besides, the reaction in most of Galilee has been very positive. In Nain, I was just hailed as 'the great eschatological prophet.' Had I had time, I would have explained to them that John is the one foretold in that role, but at least they understood that something special is happening. G-d is doing a new thing."

Jesus caught up on other news of the family. Then he walked out to where the disciples were waiting, and led them to the synagogue.

The small synagogue in Netzerit could hardly hold all the people who had gathered, the word having spread like wildfire that Jesus was back and would speak this Shabbat evening. Some of the people anticipated healings while he was present, for word of his mighty works had been heard throughout the region.

Entering the synagogue quietly, Jesus took a seat at the front with David, the synagogue ruler. The service began with prayer and some singing. Then David handed the scroll of the prophet Isaiah to Jesus. He stood at the small lectern and, unrolling the scroll to a passage near the end, he read:

> The Spirit of the Lord is on me,
>> because he has anointed me
>> to preach good news to the poor.
> He has sent me to proclaim freedom for the prisoners
>> and recovery of sight for the blind,
> to release the oppressed,
> to proclaim the year of the Lord's favor.

Jesus rolled up the scroll, gave it back to the attendant, and sat down. The eyes of everyone in the synagogue were fastened on him, as he stated, "Today this Scripture is fulfilled in your hearing."

At first, all began to speak well of him and were amazed at the gracious words that came from his lips. "Isn't this Joseph's son?" they asked.

But then Jesus said to them, "Surely you will quote this proverb to me: 'Physician, heal yourself!' You will say, 'Do here in your hometown what we have heard that you did in Kefer Nahum and in Nain.'"

He took a moment to look around the crowd, matching their eager gaze with his own before continuing. "Amen, I tell you, no prophet is accepted in his hometown. I assure you that there were many widows in Israel in Elijah's time, when the sky was shut for three and a half years and there was a severe famine throughout the land. Yet Elijah was not sent to any of them, but to a widow in Zarephath in the region of Sidon, just as I have recently helped a widow in Nain. And there were many in Israel with leprosy in the time of Elisha the prophet, yet not one of them was cleansed, only Naaman the Syrian."

The people in the synagogue were furious when they heard this, quickly understanding that Jesus meant they were as unresponsive to G-d and as stiff-necked as their forebears had been in the time of Elijah and Elisha. Further, he had intimated that he was not going to perform miracles in hard-hearted Netzerit, even though so many needed his healing touch.

So great was the animosity provoked by his words that the decorum of the service broke down. One person shouted from the back, "Is this not merely the son of Mary, of a humble carpenter's family, and are not his sisters and brothers here with us now? Who does he think he is?!"

Some of them concluded that Jesus was not merely speaking out of turn, but that he was claiming to be someone he could not possibly be—the long-awaited Messiah. Others loudly accused him of blasphemy. These men got up, and pushed Jesus out the back of the synagogue. Grabbing him by his arms, they led him out of town. They took him to the brow of the hill on which the town was built, to the very spot where Jesus had often come to pray and meditate. They intended to throw him down from the cliff top, and there begin the process of stoning him to death.

But suddenly, when the men let go of Jesus for a moment, he ceased being passive and somehow managed to walk right through the crowd and away from them all. His disciples eventually caught sight of him and ran to catch up.

"So," quipped Simon, unaware of Jesus' narrow escape, "That went well! Nothing like hometown hospitality and a warm reception."

"Too warm," replied a visibly shaken Jesus. "But it is as I stated: the saying is true, 'A prophet is not without honor except in his hometown.' And sadly amongst his own kin—even within his own home. I doubt if I shall ever be able to return home again without causing a huge problem for the rest of my family." On this somber note, Jesus turned and headed back toward Kefer Nahum. He would not frequent this part of Galilee again for a while.

The journey back to Kefer Nahum in the dark passed without incident or comment, the disciples not daring to ask Jesus what he was thinking. They now realized how serious the breach was between Jesus and Netzerit, possibly even extending to members of his own family. As they walked down the trail into the vicinity of Migdal, two men hurried toward them from the direction of Netzerit. The Twelve turned, ready for trouble, but they relaxed after they recognized the men as disciples of John.

When the two saw Jesus, they ran forward and spoke breathlessly. "John sends word from prison that he suspects his days are numbered. He wants to know for sure—as do we—*are* you the One who is to come, or should we look for another?"

The words of the prophet Isaiah, still fresh in Jesus' mind, were his response to their question. "Go and tell John again those things which you have heard about and have seen. The blind receive their sight, the lame walk, the lepers are cleansed, the deaf hear, the dead are raised up, and the poor have the good news preached to them. And blessed is the one who shall not be offended by me."

The two men looked confused, and waited for Jesus to say more. But when he did not, they nodded their heads and departed. Jesus turned to his disciples and said, "What did you go out into the wilderness to see when John was baptizing? A reed shaken by the wind? A man clothed in royal attire like Herod? Those that wear soft clothing are in kings' houses. What *did* you go out to see at the Jordan? A prophet? Yes, indeed, and I would say more than just another prophet, for this is the one of whom Isaiah wrote, 'Behold, I send my messenger before your face, which shall prepare your way before you.' From the days of John the Baptizer until now, the dominion of heaven has suffered violence and rejection, and the violent attempt to take it by force. Look at what has happened to John.

"You might well expect better of the common people, people like those in my hometown. But to what shall I compare this generation? It is like children sitting in the markets, who call out to us, saying, 'We have piped for you, and you have not danced; we have mourned with you, and you have not lamented.' For John came neither eating nor drinking, and they said, 'He has a devil.' The Son of Man came eating and drinking, and they said, 'Behold a man gluttonous, and given to too much drink, a friend of tax collectors and sinners.' But Wisdom is justified by her deeds."

The disciples had never before seen Jesus this angry—an anger toward the people of Galilee. The differences in John's and Jesus' styles of ministry had confused the people. Even the disciples were confused and afraid, because John was imprisoned and Jesus was no longer welcome in his hometown. Where was all this leading? The day had begun with exhilaration—a raising of someone from the dead, no less—but it had ended on this dark and ominous note.

17

Crossing Borders

JESUS HAD CONCLUDED that it was time to get out of Galilee for a while. Two days into their stay in Kefer Nahum, word reached them that John had been killed in brutal fashion. Herod had ordered him beheaded. Jesus, grieving the loss of his cousin, took a day apart from his disciples and headed up into the hills to pray. When he returned, he told them to pack up. Across Lake Kinneret was the region of Gerasa, Gentile territory. They would cross the lake and begin to expand the mission beyond the Holy Land.

As they made preparations, Jesus thought ahead. If things went well in Gerasa, they would try a longer trip outside the Holy Land, heading to points west and north for a while, at least until things calmed down a bit. Jesus would go across to Gerasa by boat, and after a few days, return to Kefer Nahum to leave the boats where they belonged. They would head north toward Tyre, and then east to Banyas, the town that had been renamed Caesarea Philippi. Thus they would leave Herod Antipas' territory to enter the territory of Herod Philip, who was markedly less interested in prophets and messianic figures. This would give Jesus time to teach his disciples without threats of interference from the growing number of those opposed to his proclamation of the dominion of G-d, and the deeds that accompanied his words.

As they crossed the sea that morning, James asked, "Master, explain to us one of your parables, the one about the sower." Jesus, sitting in the back of the boat on a cushion, regarded James for a moment before replying. "Very well, but let me tell the story once more to refresh it in your minds.

"A farmer went out to scatter seed. As he was scattering seed, some fell on the path; and the birds came and ate it. Other seed fell on rocky ground where the soil was shallow. Those sprouted immediately because the soil wasn't deep. When the sun came up, it scorched the plants, and they dried up because they had no roots. Other seed fell among thorny plants. The thorny plants grew and choked the seeds, and they produced nothing. Other seed fell into good soil and bore fruit. Upon growing and increasing, the seed produced in one case a yield of thirty to one, in another case a yield of sixty to one, and in another case a yield of a hundred to one. He who has ears to hear, let him hear."

"I remember the story," said James, "but what does the parable mean?"

"And," asked his brother John, "why are you willing to explain your parables to us, in private like this, but not explain them to the crowds who gather to hear you teach in Galilee? I've overheard them speaking after you tell these stories, and they seem as confused by them as we are."

"Excellent questions," said Jesus. "First of all, the secret of the dominion of G-d has been given to you. But to those on the outside everything is said in parables so that, as G-d said to Isaiah, 'they may be ever seeing but never perceiving, and ever hearing but never understanding; otherwise they might turn and be forgiven!'"

Seeing the confused expression on John's face, Jesus asked them, "Don't you understand this parable? Then how will you understand all the parables? Listen. The farmer sows the word, broadcasting the 'seed' indiscriminately. This is the meaning of the seed that fell on the path: when the word is scattered, some people hear it, and right away Satan comes and steals the word that was planted in them. Here's the meaning of the seed that fell on rocky ground: when these people hear the word, they immediately receive it joyfully. But because they have no roots, they last for only a little while. When they experience distress or abuse because of the word, they immediately fall away. Others are like the seed scattered among the thorny plants. These are the ones who have heard the word; but the worries of this life, the false appeal of wealth, and the desire for more things break in and choke the word, and it bears no fruit. The seed scattered on good soil are those who hear the word and embrace it. They bear fruit, in one case a yield of thirty to one, in another, sixty to one, and even a hundred to one."

"But," said Nathan'el, "those are impossible yields! In my best years I might hope for a thirty-to-one return on the seed I sow. But sixty? One *hundred*? That's impossible. That would change everything for farmers like myself and my neighbors. Why, I would finally be able to pay off my debts to the landowner. Maybe buy some land of my own."

Levi spoke up. "That would indeed be good news for the poor! That would truly be release for the oppressed." Jesus smiled. John shook his head, wondering, before picking up the thread of his question again.

"So what you're telling us is that not everyone will receive the good news about G-d's saving activity and respond well? That we can expect failure as well as success when we ourselves proclaim the message?"

"And," added James, "you're telling us that some who become disciples will not necessarily remain your disciples. That some will wilt when the heat is on, or fall away when under pressure, perhaps even persecution." The disciples studiously avoided making eye contact with each other after James' declaration.

"Exactly," replied Jesus, "but isn't this a commentary on what you've already seen, as well as what you can expect to see in the future?" James clearly wanted to press the matter further, but as the two boats pulled into the shallows, Jesus leapt out of the boat alongside Peter, and began to push the vessel up onto the shore. They had arrived in the Gerasene region.

As the others clambered over the sides of the boats, Jesus turned to look inland and saw a man running down the hill toward them. This man came from the tombs high up on the hillside, and as he ran he yelled at them. Jesus saw his nakedness first, and then the torment in his face.

The man lived a tortured existence among the tombs, and no one from the nearby town could bind him anymore, in their attempts to protect him from himself. He had often been chained hand and foot, but he tore the chains apart and broke the irons on his feet. No one was strong enough to subdue him. Night and day he cried out among the tombs and in the hills, and cut himself with stones.

Seeing Jesus from a distance, he ran and fell on his knees in front of him, shouting at the top of his voice, "What do you want with me, Jesus, Son of the Most High G-d? Swear to G-d that you won't torture me!" For as soon as the man fell before his feet Jesus had said, "Come out of this man, you unclean spirit!"

Jesus asked him, "What is your name?"

"My name is Legion," he replied, "for we are many." And the unclean spirits, speaking through the man, begged Jesus again and again not to send them out of the area. A large herd of pigs was feeding on the nearby hillside. The demons begged Jesus, "Send us among the pigs; allow us to go into them." He gave them permission, and the unclean spirits came out and went into the pigs. The herd, about two thousand in number, then rushed down the steep bank into the lake and drowned. Those tending the pigs ran off and reported this in the town and countryside, and the people hurried out to see what had happened.

When they came to Jesus, they saw the man who had been possessed by the legion of demons, sitting there, dressed and in his right mind; and they were afraid. Those who had seen it told the people what had happened to the demon-possessed man and about the pigs as well. Then the people began to plead with Jesus to leave their region.

With a deep sigh tinged with sadness, Jesus reluctantly saw that this trip across the sea was already at a premature end. As Jesus was getting back into the boat, the man who had been demon possessed begged to go with him. Jesus did not let him, however, but told him, "Go home to your family and tell them how much the Lord has done for you, and how he has had mercy on you." So the man went away and began to tell everyone in the Decapolis region—the ten cities that circled the sea—how much Jesus had done for him. And all the people were amazed.

"If this is the way it's going to be from now on, then it appears that the Son of Man will soon have nowhere to lay his head in peace," said Jesus, mostly to himself. The news spread right around the lake that Jesus the exorcist was doing his dramatic work both in the clean and unclean lands. When Jesus and the disciples returned to Kefer Nahum, the disciples began to realize some of the repercussions of Jesus' healings and exorcism of demons. Within only a few short days, after people had heard all that Jesus was doing, many came to him from Judaea, Yerushalayim, Idumea, and the regions across the Jordan and even from around Tyre and Sidon. Both Jews and non-Jews sought him out. And the growing presence of non-Jews disturbed some of the Jewish leaders in the area, who were especially troubled by the exorcisms. Jesus entered a house in Kefer Nahum, and again a crowd gathered, to such an extent that he and his disciples were not even able to eat.

When Jesus' family heard about all the exorcisms, healings, and the growing crowds made up of all sorts of people, they went to Kefer Nahum to take charge of him, for they said, "He is out of his mind." His brother James was especially worried that things were happening far too quickly, and that Jesus was attracting too much attention and was in danger of losing control of the situation. Before his family arrived, some teachers of the law came down from Yerushalayim to Kefer Nahum, saying, "This man is possessed by Beelzebub! By the prince of demons he is driving out demons."

Jesus could not ignore their inflammatory accusation, and responded to them in parables. "How can Satan throw Satan out? A kingdom involved in civil war will collapse. And a house torn apart by divisions will collapse. If Satan rebels against himself and is divided, then he can't endure. He's done for. No one gets into the house of a strong person and steals anything without first tying up the strong person. Only then can the house be burglarized. I assure you that human beings will be forgiven for everything, for all sins and insults of every kind. But whoever insults the Holy Spirit will never be forgiven. That person is guilty of a sin with consequences that last forever."

Then Jesus' mother and brothers arrived. Standing outside the house where Jesus said these things, they sent someone in to call for him. A crowd was sitting with him, and those standing in the doorway said, "Your mother and brothers are outside looking for you."

"Who are my mother and my brothers?" he asked. This question dumbfounded those with him, and even the disciples had no reply. Then Jesus looked at those seated in a circle around him and said, "Here are my mother and my brothers! Whoever does G-d's will is my brother and sister and mother. You may tell my mother and brothers that I am well and in my right mind. They can go back home without me now."

Naturally enough, this reply both shocked the brothers of Jesus, and disappointed them. Mary took it especially hard. Jesus was not going to cooperate and he was not going to return home with them. It was this apparent rejection that perhaps most contributed to the hardening of the heart of James and the other brothers of Jesus, who refused to join his disciples. Reminiscent of the story of Joseph with his many-colored coat and his brothers, Jesus found himself at odds with and alienated from his own family the longer his ministry lasted, and the more dramatic the results became.

After Jesus' family had reluctantly turned around and headed home again, Jesus, in his most serious and solemn manner, said to those seated with him, "Everyone who acknowledges me before people, I also will acknowledge before my Father who is in heaven. But everyone who denies me before people, I also will deny before my Father who is in heaven. Don't think that I've come to bring peace to the earth. I haven't come to bring peace but a sword. For I've come to turn 'a man against his father, a daughter against her mother, and a daughter-in-law against her mother-in-law. People's enemies are members of their own households.'" Jesus quoted these words from the prophet Micah, and to them he added, "Those who love father or mother more than me aren't worthy of me. Those who love son or daughter more than me aren't worthy of me. Those who don't pick up their crosses and follow me aren't worthy of me. Those who find their lives will lose them, but those who lose their lives because of me will find them."

Even the disciples found this hard to swallow, and one of them instantly replied, "This is a hard saying, Master. Who can accept it?" But Jesus did not reply to the rhetorical question. Instead he stood up, grabbed his traveling bag, and quietly left the house.

After this, Jesus traveled about from one town and village to another, proclaiming the good news of the dominion of G-d. The Twelve were with him, and also some women who had been cured of unclean spirits and diseases: Miryam of Migdal, from whom seven demons had come out; Joanna, the wife of Chuza, the manager of Herod's household; Susanna; and many others. These women were helping to support them out of their own means. Their presence made some of the male disciples uncomfortable, not least because most of them were married, and none of these women were their relatives. Jewish men were not normally supposed to speak to—much less travel with—women they didn't know, perhaps especially not with women like Miryam of Migdal who was widely known to have been demon possessed. They also felt uncomfortable that Jesus' benefactors—those who supported him financially—were women, which was a most undignified situation for a teacher, and by association, for them.

It was Miryam who had recruited several other women to be followers of Jesus, the most well-known of whom was Joanna, the wife of Herod's estate manager. Joanna was a well-to-do, literate woman. Miryam enlisted these women not merely so they could learn from Jesus, but because they would support his ministry. Needless to say, this traveling band created no small stir in Galilee, as it involved such a diverse group of persons: the formerly demon-possessed, fishermen, Zealots, a tax collector or two, Judaeans, Galileans, the pious, the ordinary, both men and women. If this was the guest list for the coming messianic banquet, then it surprised many who thought they knew who should be included and who should be left out.

One of the villages Jesus deliberately stopped in as he moved from place to place in Galilee was Qana, site of the family wedding he had attended months earlier. Jesus had wanted to visit in order to have more conversation with Decimus, the royal official, particularly since this man knew the Herodian clan and Jesus was contemplating visiting another Herod's territory. When he reached the man's house, however, he found it in an uproar. Something was terribly wrong: Decimus' son lay sick in Kefer Nahum. When Decimus heard that Jesus had arrived in Qana and was knocking on his door, he went to him and begged him to go to Kefer Nahum and heal the boy, who was close to death.

Jesus responded, "Unless you people see miraculous signs and wonders, you will never believe." Decimus continued to plead with Jesus, saying, "Sir, come down before my child dies." Jesus replied succinctly, "You may go to him. Your son will live."

Decimus took Jesus at his word and a few hours later, after sorting some important matters out, he departed, even though it was late in the day to be starting a journey. He traveled through the night. While he was still on the way, his servants met him with the news that his boy was living. He asked them when his son's condition had improved, and they said to him, "The fever left him yesterday at the seventh hour." Decimus realized that this was the exact time when Jesus had said to him, "Your son will live." From that day on, he and all his household believed in Jesus.

This sign happened only a few days before the Feast of Tabernacles was to be celebrated in Yerushalayim. As Jesus left Qana with his disciples, he discovered that his brothers had been told he was nearby and they came to speak with him on the road. James, along with Joses, were obviously beginning a journey somewhere as they had their traveling bags with them. James said to Jesus, "Leave Galilee and go to Judaea so that your disciples there may see the works you do. No one who wants to become a public figure acts in secret or simply tours Galilee. Since you're doing all these signs and wonders, show yourself to the world."

Jesus looked intently at James. He knew that his brothers did not believe in him, in the sense that they did not see him as the Messiah, though they knew he had performed miracles. Jesus paused to reflect on what James' motive could be for saying this. Did he want Jesus away from Galilee so things would return to normal for his family? Were they shunning him because he had not agreed to come home with them some weeks earlier? Or did James genuinely want Jesus to have more visibility, to be better known?

After a while, Jesus said to his brothers, "For you, any time is fine. But my time hasn't come yet. The world can't hate you. It hates me though, because I testify that its works are evil. You go up to the festival. I'm not going now because my time has not yet come."

Having said this, he stayed overnight in Galilee with his cousins who lived in Qana, for it was already evening. Jesus did not eat with them, but instead went out under the stars and devoted himself to prayer and reflection. The next morning, after his brothers had left for the festival, Jesus and his disciples went also—not publicly, but in secret.

As they left Qana, Simon asked, "So where shall we go now?"

"We're going to Judaea to the festival, but this time we will not travel the usual pilgrim's road along the Jordan. We will go directly south from here."

"But that way leads through Samaria!" said Simon the Zealot, protesting this route.

"Yes," replied Jesus, "and precisely for that reason it will bring us less attention. We will come back the same way after the festival, and go visit Jacob's Well."

"But Jacob's Well is near Sychar, right in the heart of Samaria!" the Zealot persisted.

"So it is Simon. So it is," Jesus replied, with an enigmatic smile.

18

The Feast of Tabernacles

THE JOURNEY THROUGH Samaria proved to be uneventful, as Jesus had suggested it would be. No one stopped them or asked anything of them, and there were no requests for miracles. They did come upon a traveler heading north, who repeated the news Jesus had already heard about Pilate's despicable act, slaughtering some Galileans so their blood mixed with the sacrifices being offered.

After hearing the grim report again, Jesus asked his disciples: "Do you think that those Galileans were worse sinners than all the other Galileans, because they suffered this way? I tell you, no! But unless you repent, you too will all perish. Or those eighteen who died when the tower in Siloam recently fell on them. Do you think they were more guilty than all the others living in Yerushalayim? I tell you, no! But unless you repent, you too will all perish."

This teaching frightened the traveler, but Jesus wasn't finished. He told the traveler a parable. "A man had a fig tree planted in his vineyard, and he went to look for fruit on it, but did not find any. So he said to the man who took care of the vineyard, 'For three years now I've been coming to look for fruit on this fig tree and haven't found any. Cut it down! Why should it use up the soil?' 'Sir,' the man replied, 'leave it alone for one more year, and I'll dig around it and fertilize it. If it bears fruit next year, fine! If not, then cut it down.'"

The traveler was a fellow Galilean. As he reflected on Jesus' words, he said, "So are you saying that unless there is change in Judaea, G-d will soon judge the population, and their rulers? For surely the image of the vineyard refers to Judaea."

"You have spoken well," responded Jesus. "Go on your way. Shalom to you and your family."

The disciples were quiet as they continued down the road, ruminating on what Jesus had said. On the one hand, Jesus was going through Samaria, the apparently safer route south. But on the other hand, he *was* going to Judaea and Yerushalayim, where the most intense scrutiny would fall upon him if he taught or healed in public. Even Nathan'el, the diligent student of Torah, could not figure out Jesus' thinking in all this. Did Jesus *want* to provoke a confrontation in Yerushalayim? It was deeply puzzling.

Jesus now turned to Nathan'el. "Tell us the story of the Feast of Tabernacles," he said. "What do we hear in Torah?"

"As you know, Master, the Feast of Tabernacles is a week-long autumn harvest festival, which is also known as the Feast of the Ingathering, the Feast of Booths, or Sukkoth. The Feast of Tabernacles is the final and most important and joyous holiday of the year, for it is our harvest festival. The importance of this festival is indicated by the statement, 'This is to be a lasting ordinance.' The divine pronouncement, 'I am the Lord your G-d,' concludes this section on the holidays of the seventh month. The Feast of Tabernacles begins five days after Yom Kippur, the day of Atonement, on the fifteenth of Tishri.

"The word *Sukkoth*, of course, means 'booths,' and refers to the temporary dwellings that we are commanded to live in during this holiday, just as our ancestors did in the wilderness. Torah says about its celebration that we should keep this festival, 'That your generations may know that I made the children of Israel to dwell in booths, when I brought them out of the land of Egypt: I am the LORD your G-d.' In short, it is a reminder of when we were in transition and had no permanent home in the land."

"It is good that we have a Scripture scholar in our midst," said Jesus, "and I have a question for you. Why do you think I told the story about the unfruitful tree as we head to a harvest festival, and what do you think G-d wants us to remember by having us celebrate in temporary dwellings?"

Nathan'el cleared his throat and spoke once more, his expression thoughtful. "Perhaps because G-d wants to remind us that the only permanent thing is our dependence on and relationship with him, blessed be he. And it seems to me you are suggesting that to whom more is given, more is required, for indeed, judgment begins with the household of G-d."

"Yes," said Jesus, "and not merely on G-d's own people, but on G-d's own house."

"But it's not even finished yet," said Simon, referring to Herod's temple.

"What is it that the psalmist says?" replied Jesus. "'Unless the Lord builds your house, you labor in vain.'"

As Jesus and the disciples came within sight of Bet Anya, Jesus sent Simon and Andrew ahead to let Mary, Martha, and Lazarus know they were nearby. The plan was for the disciples to camp out on the land behind their house. The family in Bet Anya was overjoyed to see Jesus again, and the disciples clearly saw just how much Jesus loved this family. During the days they spent enjoying the family's generous hospitality, they noticed the obvious affection Jesus held for Lazarus, who often reclined beside him at meals. After a few days of rest and conversation, Jesus said to his disciples, "Come, it is time for me to go to Yerushalayim to teach in the temple precincts."

"I would not advise it, Master," said Martha. "There are many, many people in the city who have serious doubts about you, questioning whether you are a good Jew. And as is always the case, the vast crowds of pilgrims have the authorities on edge. The Romans' hands rest uneasily on their swords."

Jesus simply smiled and said, "Martha, Martha, once again you are worried about many things, but I must concentrate on the one thing that is necessary."

And with that he made his way out of the house and headed down the road to the Kidron in order to enter the city and climb up the hill called Zion to the temple itself. Many of the disciples gaped at the sights of the temple as they made their way to Jesus' customary spot for teaching. Those from Galilee were especially stunned by the size and scope of the temple complex even though it was still under construction, employing about half of Yerushalayim's workforce. Some of the beveled stones that went into the temple mount itself were as large as a small house in Netzerit, and it was amazing to watch such enormous stones being lowered into place, one on top of another.

They paused to watch as some engineers oversaw the lowering of one of these massive blocks of stone into place. Lead and sand was placed on the top portion of the stone already in place so that the stone that was about to be lowered would not crack or break the one beneath it. The lead cushioned the blow of the stone, which must have easily weighed more than a ton. Once the stone was in place, the workers blew the sand out from between the stones. Jesus pointed to one stone on the ground next to the temple mount, apparently rejected by the architects because they had found some flaw in it.

"What is it that the psalmist says?" asked Jesus. "'The stone that the builders have rejected has become the main cornerstone.' Even so it will be in my case." But none of the disciples remarked on Jesus' statement, they were so captivated by the size and scope of everything they were seeing.

Jesus did not teach that day. In fact, it was not until halfway through the festival week that Jesus returned to the temple courts and began teaching the crowds. The Jewish officials were amazed and asked, "How did this man get such learning without having studied?" By this they meant that Jesus had never come to Yerushalayim to study with their scribes, sages, or teachers.

Jesus, knowing exactly what they were thinking, answered, "My teaching isn't mine, but comes from the One who sent me. Whoever wants to do the will of G-d will find out whether my teaching is from G-d or whether I speak on my own. Those who speak on their own seek glory for themselves. But he who seeks the glory of the One who sent him is a person of truth; there is no falsehood in him. Did not Moses give you the Law? Yet none of you keep the Law. Why do you want to kill me?"

The crowd answered, "You must have a demon! Who wants to kill you?"

Jesus replied, "I did a miracle or two on Shabbat, and you were all astonished. Because Moses gave you the commandment about circumcision—although it wasn't Moses but the patriarchs—you circumcise a boy on Shabbat. If a boy can be circumcised on Shabbat without breaking Moses' Law, why are you angry with me because I made an entire man well on Shabbat? Don't judge according to appearances. Judge with right judgment."

At this point some of the people of Yerushalayim said, "Isn't he the one they want to kill? Yet here he is, speaking in public, and they aren't saying anything to him. Could it be that our leaders actually think he *is* the Messiah? We know where this man is from, but when the Messiah comes, no one will know where he is from."

As Jesus continued to teach in the temple, he exclaimed, "You know me and where I am from. I haven't come on my own. The One who sent me is true, but you don't know him. I know him because I am from him and he sent me." At this, they wanted to seize Jesus, but they couldn't because his time had not yet come.

Still, many from that crowd believed in Jesus. They said, "When the Messiah comes, will he do more miraculous signs than this man does?" The Pharisees heard the crowd whispering such things about Jesus, and the chief priest and Pharisees sent guards to arrest him.

Jesus told them all, "I am with you for only a short time, and then I go to the One who sent me. You will look for me, but you will not find me; and where I am, you cannot come."

The Jewish officials present said to one another, "Where does this man intend to go that we cannot find him? Will he go where our people live scattered among the Greeks, and teach the Greeks? What did he mean when he said, 'You will look for me, but you will not find me,' and 'Where I am, you cannot come'?" Jesus, of course, had in mind not merely the trip he planned north of Galilee, but something more.

The disciples were alarmed by the confrontation they witnessed in the temple courts, but they left quietly with Jesus and returned to Bet Anya. Jesus did not return to the temple that day or the next. But on the last and greatest day of the feast, Jesus returned to the same spot where he had taught, in the Court of the Gentiles, and stood and said in a loud voice, "All who are thirsty should come to me! All who believe in me should drink! As the Scriptures said concerning me, 'Rivers of living water will flow out from within him.'" Jesus said this concerning the Spirit. Those who believed in him would soon receive the Spirit, but they hadn't experienced the Spirit yet, since Jesus had not yet been glorified.

When some in the crowd heard these words, they said, "This man is truly the prophet." Others said, "He's the Messiah." But others said, "The Messiah can't come from Galilee, can he? Didn't the Scriptures say that the Christ comes from David's family and from Bet Lehem, David's village?" So the crowd was divided over Jesus. Some wanted to arrest him, but no one seized him.

Finally, the temple guards went back, without Jesus, to the chief priests and Pharisees. They questioned the guards, saying, "Why didn't you bring him in?"

The guards responded, "No one ever spoke the way this man does."

The Pharisees retorted, "Have you too been deceived? Have any of the leaders believed in him? Has any Pharisee? No, only this crowd, which does not know the Law. And they are under G-d's curse!" Nicodemus was present, and said, "Our Law doesn't judge someone without first hearing him and learning what he is doing, does it?"

They answered him mockingly. "You are not from Galilee too, are you? Look it up and you will see that the prophet does not come from Galilee." They were bitterly divided over Jesus. But Jesus himself, knowing what was in their hearts, had already left the temple precincts, collected his disciples, and told them, "It's time to head north again, back through Samaria. We're finished here for a while."

"If you say so, Master," replied Simon, who was looking forward to getting out of volatile Yerushalyim and heading to Samaria, where he knew few would think to look for them.

19

The Woman at the Well

JESUS AND HIS disciples spent the night on the road, and after a morning's walk in grueling heat, they arrived at a town in Samaria called Sychar. Jacob's Well was just outside the walls, the town's water source taking its name from the plot of ground Jacob had given to his son Joseph on this spot. Jesus, tired as he was from the journey, sat down by the well. It was about the sixth hour, midday. Within sight of this well was Mount Gerizim, the holy mountain where the Samaritans offered sacrifices and celebrated Passover.

His disciples had gone into the town to buy food, leaving Jesus sitting in the shade of a tree by the well. A village woman came to draw water. Jesus said to her, "Give me some water to drink."

The Samaritan woman, pointing out the obvious, said, "Why do you, a Jewish man, ask for something to drink from me, a Samaritan woman?" Jews normally will not share a common cup with Samaritans.

Jesus responded, "If you recognized G-d's gift and who it is who is saying to you, 'Give me some water to drink,' you would be asking him and he would give you living water."

"Sir, you don't have a bucket and the well is deep. Where would you get this living water? You aren't greater than our father Jacob, are you? He gave this well to us, and he drank from it himself, as did his sons and his livestock."

"Everyone who drinks this water will be thirsty again, but whoever drinks from the water that I give will never be thirsty again. The water that I give will become in those who drink it a spring of water that bubbles up into eternal life."

"Sir, give me this water, so that I will never be thirsty and will never need to come here to draw water!"

Jesus regarded her for a moment before saying, "Go, get your husband, and come back here."

The woman replied curtly, turning her reddening face away from him, "I don't have a husband."

"You are right to say, 'I don't have a husband.' The fact is, you've had five husbands, and the man you are with now isn't your husband. You've spoken the truth."

"Sir, I see that you are a prophet." Seeking to change the subject, she added, "Our ancestors worshiped on this mountain, but you and your people say that it is necessary to worship in Yerushalayim."

"Believe me, woman, the time is coming when you and your people will worship the Father neither on this mountain nor in Yerushalayim. You and your people worship what you don't know; we worship what we know because salvation is from the Jews. But the time is coming—and is here!—when true worshipers will worship in spirit and in truth. The Father looks for those who worship him this way. G-d is spirit, and it is necessary to worship G-d in spirit and truth."

The woman looked curiously at Jesus, and then said, "I know that the Messiah is coming, the One who is called the Christ. When he comes, he will teach us everything."

Jesus smiled at her unspoken question, and responded, "I—the One who speaks with you—I am he."

Just then, Jesus' disciples arrived and were shocked that he was talking with a woman. But no one dared to ask, "What do you want?" or "Why are you talking with her?"

The woman put down her water jar and ran back into the town. She said to the people, "Come and see a man who has told me everything I've done! Could this man be the Messiah?" They left the city and made their way out to see Jesus.

Meanwhile the disciples urged Jesus, "Teacher, eat."

Jesus said to them, "I have food to eat that you don't know about."

The disciples asked each other, "Has someone brought him food?"

Jesus said to them, "I am fed by doing the will of the One who sent me and by completing his work. Don't you have a saying, 'Four more months and then it's time for harvest'? Look, I tell you: open your eyes and notice that the fields are already ripe for the harvest. Those who harvest are receiving their pay and gathering fruit for eternal life, so that those who sow and those who harvest can celebrate together. This is a true saying, that one sows and another harvests. I have sent you to harvest what you didn't work hard for; others worked hard, and you will share in their hard work."

Many Samaritans in that town believed in Jesus because of the woman's word when she testified, "He told me everything I've ever done." So when the Samaritans came to Jesus, they asked him to stay with them, and he stayed there two days. Many more believed because of his word, and they said to the woman, "We no longer believe because of what you said, for we have heard for ourselves and know that this one is truly the savior of the world."

The disciples hardly knew what to make of all this. They had just seen Jesus violently opposed by his fellow Jews in Yerushalayim, but now fully welcomed by Samaritans. What manner of Messiah could Jesus be? As Jesus and the disciples headed back north to Galilee, there was much to ponder.

Once they crossed into Galilee, the word quickly spread that Jesus was back in his home region, and many came out to entreat him for healing or some other form of help. As they headed into the hill country near Netzerit, a man ran up to Jesus and fell on his knees before him. "Good teacher," he asked, "what must I do to inherit everlasting life?"

"Why do you call me good?" replied Jesus. "No one is good except the one G-d. You know the commandments: You shall not commit murder. You shall not commit adultery. You shall not steal. You shall not give false testimony. You shall not cheat. Honor your father and mother."

"Teacher," the man responded earnestly, "I've kept all of these things since I was a boy."

Jesus looked at him intently and loved him. "Then you are lacking one thing. Go, sell what you own, and give the money to the poor. Then you will have treasure in heaven. And come, follow me!" But the man was dismayed at this statement and went away saddened, because he had many possessions.

Jesus turned to his disciples. "It will be very hard for the wealthy to enter G-d's dominion." His words startled the disciples, so Jesus told them again, "Children, it is difficult to enter G-d's dominion! It's easier for a camel to squeeze through the eye of a needle than for a rich person to enter G-d's dominion."

They were shocked at this. Surely the wealthy were the ones who were able to be truly pious, having the time and resources to engage in the sanctioned acts of piety: regular prayer, the giving of alms. They said to each other, "Then who can be saved?"

Jesus looked at them intently and said, "It's impossible with human beings, but not with G-d. All things are possible for G-d."

Peter blurted out, "Look, *we've* left everything and followed you."

"Yes," said Jesus, "and I assure you that anyone who has left house, brothers, sisters, mother, father, children, or farms because of me and because of the good news will receive a hundred times as much now in this life: houses, brothers, sisters, mothers, children, and farms—with persecutions, mind you—and in the coming age, eternal life. But many who are first will be last. And many who are last will be first."

At this point, the disciples were too weary and hungry to worry about the meaning of these words or to ask questions as the sun went down. *At least*, they thought, *we're back in Galilee.*

20

The Sermon on the Mount

THEY HAD SPENT some time in the region around Gennesaret, on the northwest shore of Lake Kinneret. Many had come seeking healing, and as the disciples observed Jesus' tender care and concern for the poor, the diseased and the demonized, they began to feel uneasy. Surely G-d was with their Master, and when the Messiah came, would he do more than Jesus had already done? Yet they were bothered that Jesus seemed to have alienated not only his family and hometown folks, but many among the Jewish authorities as well. They expressed their concern to each other in whispered voices. They wondered where all this was leading. Jesus was well aware of their concerns and he continued to instruct them, that they might grow in their understanding.

This particular day had begun innocently enough, with Jesus eating with his disciples. But Jesus and the disciples were never alone anymore, whether they were in Galilee or Judaea, and among those present were some Pharisees and their scribes who taught Torah. They had come to Galilee from Yerushalayim after his recent visit there. They saw some of his disciples eating food with hands that were "unclean," that is, unwashed. Offended by this lack of piety, the Pharisees and scribes asked Jesus, "Why don't your disciples live according to the tradition of the elders, instead of eating their food with unclean hands?"

Jesus sighed wearily, and responded bluntly. "Isaiah was right when he prophesied about you hypocrites, as it is written: 'These people honor me with their lips, but their hearts are far from me. They worship me in vain; their teachings are but rules taught by men.'"

He continued: "You ignore G-d's commandment while holding on to rules created by mere mortals and handed down to you. Clearly, you are experts at rejecting G-d's commandment in order to establish your own rules. For Moses said, 'Honor your father and your mother' and, 'The person who speaks against father or mother will certainly be put to death.' But you say, 'If you tell your father or mother, "Everything I'm expected to contribute to you is *corban*, that is, a gift I'm giving to G-d," then you are no longer required to care for your father or mother.' In this way you do away with G-d's word in favor of the rules handed down to you, which you pass on to others. And you do a lot of things just like that."

Addressing not only his inquisitors but also his disciples and others gathered there, Jesus said, "Listen to me, all of you, and understand. Nothing outside of a person can enter and contaminate a person in G-d's sight; rather, the things that come *out* of a person contaminate the person." These responses clearly did nothing to placate the Pharisees, who saw Jesus as not merely setting aside the traditions of the elders, but setting aside some of Torah itself. However, Jesus didn't wait around for the Pharisees' rebuttal.

He left the crowd and entered the home of Simon's mother-in-law, where his disciples asked him about this parable. He said to them, "Don't you understand either? Don't you know that nothing from the outside that enters a person has the power to contaminate? That's because it doesn't enter into the heart but into the stomach, and it goes out into the sewer." By saying this, Jesus declared that no food could contaminate a person in G-d's sight. "It's what comes out of a person that contaminates someone in G-d's sight. It's from the inside, from the human heart, that evil thoughts come: sexual sins, thefts, murders, adultery, greed, evil actions, deceit, unrestrained immorality, envy, insults, arrogance, and foolishness. All these evil things come from the inside and contaminate a person in G-d's sight."

The disciples listened intently, but Nathan'el replied, "Master, even if what you say is true, do we really need to alienate the Pharisees and their scribes? They're well respected by the people." Jesus looked at Nathan'el intently, then around at the other disciples. There was so much they needed to understand, so much that would stand in stark contrast to the teaching of the scribes and Pharisees. Yet the message of the dominion of G-d was indeed *good* news—and not just for his disciples. It was good news for whoever had ears to hear. With that thought, Jesus said to his disciples, "Follow me."

The very minute Jesus came out of the house, the crowds outside began clamoring for attention. But with a look of determination, Jesus headed out of town and up the hill. He led them around the northern tip of the lake, going to a large bowl-shaped meadow on the northeast side of the Kinneret, where he knew the sound of his voice could be heard throughout the meadow. Sitting on a flat, moss-covered rock, Jesus surveyed the crowds as they began to fan out in concentric circles around the disciples, crowding in so they could hear more clearly. Looking at his disciples, but speaking loudly enough so that all could hear, Jesus began to teach them, saying:

Blessed are the poor in spirit,
    for theirs is the kingdom of heaven.
Blessed are those who mourn,
    for they will be comforted.
Blessed are the meek,
    for they will inherit the earth.
Blessed are those who hunger and thirst for righteousness,
    for they will be filled.
Blessed are the merciful,
    for they will be shown mercy.
Blessed are the pure in heart,
    for they will see G-d.
Blessed are the peacemakers,
    for they will be called sons of G-d.
Blessed are those who are persecuted because of righteousness,
    for theirs is the kingdom of heaven.
Blessed are you when men insult you, persecute you, and
falsely say all kinds of evil against you because of me.
Rejoice and be glad, because great is your reward in heaven,
for in the same way, they persecuted the prophets who
were before you.

"You are the salt of the earth. But if salt loses its saltiness, how will it become salty again? It's good for nothing except to be thrown away and trampled under people's feet. You are the light of the world. A city on top of a hill can't be hidden. Neither do people light a lamp and put it under a basket. Instead, they put it on top of a lampstand, and it shines on all who are in the house. In the same way, let your light shine before people, so they can see the good things you do and praise your Father who is in heaven.

"Don't even begin to think that I have come to do away with the Law and the Prophets. I haven't come to do away with them but to fulfill them. I say to you very seriously that as long as heaven and earth exist, neither the smallest letter nor even the smallest stroke of a pen will be erased from the Law until everything there becomes a reality. Therefore, whoever ignores one of the least of these commands and teaches others to do the same will be called the lowest in the kingdom of heaven. But whoever keeps these commands and teaches people to keep them will be called great in the kingdom of heaven. I say to you that unless your righteousness is greater than the righteousness of the legal experts and the Pharisees, you will never enter the kingdom of heaven.

"You have heard that it was said to those who lived long ago, 'You shouldn't commit murder, and all who commit murder will be in danger of judgment.' But I say to you that everyone who is *angry* with their brother or sister will be in danger of judgment. If they say to their brother or sister, '*Raca*,' calling them an idiot, then they will be in danger of being condemned by the governing council. And if they say, 'You fool,' they will be in danger of the fires of Gehenna.[1] Therefore, if you bring your gift to the altar and there

---

1. The Aramaic word "Gehenna" is the equivalent of the word "Hinnom," referring to the valley on the south side of the city of David in Jerusalem where garbage was burned in Jesus' day. In an earlier era, it had also been the place where children were sacrificed to the god Molech. In other words, this place had only terrible associations in the minds of Jews. As a garbage dump, it was

remember that your brother or sister has something against you, leave your gift at the altar and go. First make things right with your brother or sister, and then come back and offer your gift. Be sure to make friends quickly with your opponents while you are on the way to court with them. Otherwise, they will haul you before the judge, the judge will turn you over to the officer of the court, and you will be thrown into prison. I say to you in all seriousness that you won't get out of there until you've paid the very last penny.

"You have heard that it was said, 'Do not commit adultery.' But I tell you that anyone who looks at a woman lustfully has already committed adultery with her in his heart. And if your right eye causes you to fall into sin, tear it out and throw it away. It's better that you lose a part of your body than that your whole body be thrown into Gehenna. And if your right hand causes you to fall into sin, chop it off and throw it away. It's better that you lose a part of your body than that your whole body go into Gehenna.

"It has been said, 'Anyone who divorces his wife must give her a certificate of divorce.' But I tell you that anyone who divorces his wife, except on grounds of incest,[2] causes her to become an adulteress, and anyone who marries the divorced woman commits adultery.

"Again, you have heard that it was said to those who lived long ago, 'You shouldn't swear a false oath, but you should follow

a place where the maggots were always busy, and the fires always smoldered, which is precisely why Jesus uses this grisly image to characterize what we would call hell, the place of eternal punishment.

2. Divorce was a political hot potato at the time, because Herod Antipas had married his brother's wife, a relationship John himself had critiqued, and which probably led to John's execution at Antipas' orders. This may well have been the backdrop to Jesus' teaching here.

through on what you have sworn to the Lord.' But I say to you that you must not swear at all. You must not swear by heaven, because it is G-d's throne. You must not swear by the earth, because it is G-d's footstool. You must not swear by Yerushalayim, because it is the city of the Great King. And you must not swear by your head, because you can't turn one hair white or black. Let your 'yes' mean 'yes,' and your 'no' mean 'no.' Anything more than this comes from the Evil One.

"You have heard that it was said, 'An eye for an eye and a tooth for a tooth.' But I say to you that you must not oppose those who want to hurt you. If people slap you on your right cheek, you must turn the left cheek to them as well. When they wish to haul you to court and take your shirt, let them have your coat too. When they force you to go one mile, go with them two. Give to those who ask, and don't refuse those who wish to borrow from you.

"You have heard that it was said, 'You should love your neighbor and hate your enemy.' But I say to you, love your enemies, and pray for those who harass you because of your faith, so that you will be acting as children of your Father who is in heaven. For he makes the sun rise on both the evil and the good, and sends rain on both the righteous and the unrighteous. If you love only those who love you, what reward do you have? Don't even the tax collectors do the same? And if you greet only your brothers and sisters, what more are you doing? Don't even the pagans do the same? Therefore, just as your heavenly Father is perfect in showing love to everyone, so also you must be perfect.

"Be careful that you don't practice your religion in front of people to draw their attention. If you do, you will have no reward from your Father who is in heaven. Whenever you give to the poor, don't blow your trumpet as the hypocrites do in the syna-gogues and in the streets, so that they may get praise from people. I assure you, that's the only reward they'll get. But when you give to the poor, don't let your left hand know what your right hand is doing, so that you may give to the poor in secret. Your Father who sees what you do in secret will reward you.

"When you pray, don't be like the hypocrites. They love to pray standing in the synagogues and on the street corners, so that people will see them. I assure you, that's the only reward they'll get. But when you pray, go to your room, shut the door, and pray to your Father who is present in that secret place. Your Father who sees what you do in secret will reward you. And when you pray, do not keep on babbling like the pagans, for they think they will be heard because of their many words. Don't be like them, for your Father knows what you need before you ask him. This, then, is how you should pray:

> Abba,
> may your name be hallowed,
> your dominion come,
> your will be done
>   on earth as it is in heaven.
> Give us today our daily bread.
> Forgive us our debts,
>   as we also have forgiven our debtors.
> And lead us not into temptation,
> but deliver us from the evil one.

"For if you forgive people when they sin against you, your heavenly Father will also forgive you. But if you do not forgive men their sins, your Father will not forgive your sins.

"And when you fast, don't put on a sad face like the hypocrites. They distort their faces so people will know they are fasting. I assure you that they have their reward. When you fast, brush your hair and wash your face. Then you won't look like you are fasting to people, but only to your Father, who is present in that secret place. Your Father, who sees in secret, will reward you.

"Do not store up for yourselves treasures on earth, where moth and rust destroy, and where thieves break in and steal. But store up for yourselves treasures in heaven, where moth and rust do not destroy, and where thieves do not break in and steal. For where your treasure is, there your heart will be also.

"The eye is the lamp of the body. Therefore, if your eye is healthy, your whole body will be full of light. But if your eye is bad, your whole body will be full of darkness. If then the light in you is darkness, how terrible that darkness will be! No one can serve two masters. Either you will hate the one and love the other, or you will be loyal to the one and have contempt for the other. You cannot serve G-d and Mammon.[3]

"Therefore, I say to you, don't worry about your life, what you'll eat or what you'll drink, or about your body, what you'll wear. Isn't life more than food and the body more than clothes? Look at the birds in the sky. They don't sow seed or harvest grain or gather crops into barns. Yet your heavenly Father feeds them. Aren't you worth much more than they are? Who among you, by worrying, can add a single moment to your life? And why do you worry about clothes? Notice how the flowers in the field grow. They

---

3. It is uncertain as to whether "Mammon" is simply Jesus' term for money in general, or if it refers to wealth, or treasure on earth, as Jesus has already called it.

don't wear themselves out with work, and they don't spin cloth. But I say to you that even Solomon in all of his splendor wasn't dressed like one of these. If G-d dresses grass in the field so beautifully, even though it's alive today and tomorrow it's thrown into the furnace, won't G-d do much more for you, you people of weak faith? Therefore, don't worry and say, 'What are we going to eat?' or, 'What are we going to drink?' or, 'What are we going to wear?' Pagans long for all these things. Your heavenly Father knows that you need them. Instead, seek first and foremost G-d's dominion and G-d's righteousness, and all these things will be given to you as well. Therefore, stop worrying about tomorrow, because tomorrow will worry about itself. Each day has enough trouble of its own."

As Jesus continued to teach the crowds, the disciples began to exchange sideways glances. This teaching was almost as confusing as the parables. Some of it almost sounded like Jesus was contradicting Torah, or at least setting some parts of it aside. And what did he mean when he said he had come to "fulfill" the Law? Judas and Simon the Zealot had looked at each other during Jesus' comments about loving one's enemies, even praying for one's persecutors. How could the Messiah lead resistance against the Romans if violent means were not an option? How could lust in the heart be the same as committing adultery? And divorce would no longer be an option for disgruntled husbands, at least for those who wanted to enter the dominion of G-d? This teaching raised as many questions as it gave answers. Several of the disciples found themselves staring at the ground, shaking their heads. But if Jesus noticed this, he gave no indication as he continued teaching.

"Don't condemn others, and G-d won't condemn you. G-d will be as hard on you as you are on others! He will treat you exactly as you treat them. You can see the speck in your friend's eye, but you don't notice the log in your own eye. How can you say, 'My friend, let me take the speck out of your eye,' when you don't see the log in your own eye? You're nothing but show-offs! First, take the log out of your own eye. Then you can see how to take the speck out of your friend's eye.

"Don't give to dogs what belongs to G-d. They will only turn and attack you. Don't throw pearls down in front of pigs. They will trample all over them. Ask, and you will receive. Search, and you will find. Knock, and the door will be opened for you. Everyone who asks will receive. Everyone who searches will find. And the door will be opened for everyone who knocks. Would any of you give your hungry child a stone, if the child asked for some bread? Would you give your child a snake if the child asked for a fish? As bad as you are, you still know how to give good gifts to your children. But your heavenly Father is even more ready to give good things to people who ask.

"Treat others as you want them to treat you. This is what the Law and the Prophets are all about. Go in through the narrow gate. The gate to destruction is wide, and the road that leads there is easy to follow. A lot of people go through that gate. But the gate to life is very narrow. The road that leads there is so hard to follow that only a few people find it.

"Watch out for false prophets! They dress up like sheep, but inside they are wolves who have come to attack you. You can tell what they are by what they do. No one picks grapes or figs from thornbushes. A good tree produces good fruit, and a bad tree produces bad fruit. A good tree cannot produce bad fruit, and a bad tree cannot produce good fruit. Every tree that produces bad fruit will be chopped down and burned. You can tell who the false prophets are by their deeds. Not everyone who calls me their Master will get into the kingdom of heaven. Only the ones who obey my Father in heaven will get in. On the day of judgment, many will call me their Master. They will say, 'We preached in your name, and in your name we forced out demons and worked many miracles.' But I will tell them, 'I will have nothing to do with you! Get out of my sight, you evil people!'

"Anyone who hears and obeys these teachings of mine is like a wise person who built a house on solid rock. Rain poured down, rivers flooded, and winds beat against that house. But it did not fall, because it was built on solid rock. Anyone who hears my teachings and doesn't obey them is like a foolish person who built a house on sand. The rain poured down, the rivers flooded, and the winds blew and beat against that house. Finally, it fell with a crash."

Jesus taught into the afternoon, and the heat of the day began to affect the crowds on the hillside. Most of them had followed Jesus with no thought about food and drink, and now they were hungry for more than words. Jesus looked at the crowd, which now seemed to number in the thousands, and felt compassion in his heart, because they hungered for the truth about G-d, but were like sheep without a shepherd.

As the sun began to set, his disciples came to him. "This is a remote place, and it's already very late. Send the people away so they can go to the surrounding countryside and villages and buy themselves something to eat." But Jesus answered, "*You* give them something to eat."

Judas exclaimed, "That would take eight months of a man's wages! Are we to go and spend that much on bread and give it to them to eat?"

"How many loaves do you have?" asked Jesus. "Go and see."
When they found out, they said, "Five, and two fish."

Then Jesus directed the disciples to have the people sit down in groups on the grass. So they sat down in groups of hundreds and fifties. Taking the five loaves and the two fish, and looking up to heaven, Jesus gave thanks and broke the loaves. Then he gave them to his disciples to set before the people. He also divided the two fish among them all. They all ate and were satisfied, and the disciples picked up twelve basketfuls of broken pieces of bread and fish. The number of the men who had eaten was five thousand, not counting the numerous women and children as well.

As the crowd was eating, Jesus decided it was time to leave. He told his disciples to head to the lakeshore, where several boats were anchored. He gave them instructions to get in one of the boats and go on ahead of him to Bet Saida, while he dismissed the crowd. After doing so, he went up on the mountainside to pray.

Although the sun had been low on the horizon, the disciples had been in no hurry to row across the northern part of the lake. Now the wind had suddenly picked up. When night fell, the boat was in the middle of the lake. From his vantage point high on the hill above, Jesus saw the disciples straining at the oars, because the wind was against them. Jesus went down to the lakeshore and then out to them, walking on the lake. He was about to pass by them, but when they saw him walking on the lake they thought he was a ghost. They cried out, because they all saw him and were terrified. Immediately, he spoke to them and said, "Take courage! It is I. Don't be afraid." Then he climbed into the boat with them, and the wind immediately died down. They were completely dumbfounded, for they had not understood what the multiplication of the loaves had suggested about Jesus' identity, because their hearts were hardened. When they had crossed over, they landed back at Gennesaret and anchored there.

As soon as they got out of the boat, people immediately recognized Jesus. They ran throughout that whole region and carried the sick on mats to wherever they heard he was. As he made his way to Bet Saida, when he passed through villages, towns, or the countryside, they placed the sick in the market places. They begged him to let them touch even the edge of his cloak, and all who touched him were healed.

Some people brought a blind man and begged Jesus to touch him. He took the blind man by the hand and led him outside his village. When he had spit on the man's eyes and put his hands on him, Jesus asked, "Do you see anything?" The man looked up and said, "I see people; they look like trees walking around." Once more Jesus put his hands on the man's eyes. Then his eyes were opened, his sight was restored, and he saw everything clearly. Jesus sent him home, saying, "Don't go into the village here. People will have too many questions and won't leave you alone."

It was nearly midnight when Jesus finally reached Bet Saida and retreated indoors into Simon's own house. As they were bedding down for the night, he turned to Simon and said, "We will head north in the morning. There are more things you need to know about me. And about yourself." By this time Simon had learned to expect such vague statements from Jesus, and as he was too tired to question him, he simply replied, "Yes, Master. Sleep well."

21

Revelations and Riddles

JESUS ROSE BEFORE dawn, and Simon found him eating a crust of bread and drinking some water from the well in the courtyard. The other disciples had spread themselves out among the houses of James and John, Simon and Andrew and Philip, all of whom called Bet Saida home. Simon could see that Jesus was eager to get moving, and so he washed his face at the well and started waking the other disciples, then went down the lane to James and John's house to get them started as well. Within an hour all of them had broken fast, washed, and packed food for the road. They headed out, Jesus taking them north by northwest, along some of the major roads. It was clear they would be leaving Galilee and heading into the province of Syria—their first journey beyond the ancient borders of Israel. The journey took all that day and well into the next one, and the disciples grew tired from trudging along, mile after mile.

They had just entered the district of Tyre and Sidon when a Canaanite woman came to Jesus, crying out, "Master, Son of David, have mercy on me! My daughter is tormented terribly by a demon." But Jesus did not respond to her pleas.

The disciples urged him, "Send her away; she keeps shouting out after us."

Jesus looked at them and said, "I've been sent only to the lost sheep of the people of Israel." The disciples nodded at Jesus' apparent agreement with their sentiment that they shouldn't be bothered by this Gentile woman and her needs. Was not their mission to their own people, just as Jesus had remarked? Yet if that was the case, why were they here?

The woman, however, was undeterred by Jesus' seemingly cold words. She came and knelt before him. "Master, help me!"

Jesus looked at her intently before saying, "It is not right to take the children's bread and toss it to dogs."

Without hesitating she shot back, "Yes, sir, but even the dogs eat the crumbs that fall off their master's table."

At this remark, Jesus turned to the disciples and questioningly raised an eyebrow before turning back to the woman, who lay prostrate at his feet. "Woman, you have great faith! Your request is granted." And right then, her daughter was healed.

The disciples shared uneasy glances. Many of them had a feeling that they had just been tested by Jesus, and had somehow failed in their response to her request. Jesus was continually crossing social boundaries, and crossing this geographical boundary further underlined that. What were they supposed to learn from this incident?

They set off once more, and after a while came to a fork in the road. Jesus made an unexpected right turn, which would take them into the territory of Herod Philip, on a road that led to Banyas, or Caesarea Philippi, and not on to Tyre as they had presumed. He seemed to be moving with purpose, and with some haste.

After a night out in the open, and another day of walking, they finally arrived in Banyas, an ancient Greek city full of prominently displayed idols. Herod Philip had turned the city into his showpiece, naming it after both himself and Caesar. The most recent addition was a temple built for the Imperial cult—worship of the emperor.

There was an enormous cave at Caesarea Philippi, which, when the city had been Greek, was called the Cave of Pan. Some even said that it was a gateway into the underworld. But whatever it was, the place seemed quite foreboding despite the pleasant, bubbling spring nearby. Having reached the very center of the city, Jesus and his disciples sat down at the edge of the square across from both the cave and the honorific wall full of niches containing statues of gods and men. The disciples felt overwhelmed in this pagan place. It seemed so different from their home villages. Suddenly, Jesus turned and asked them directly, "What are you hearing? Who do people say the Son of Man is?"

They looked at each other before answering his question. "Some say John the Baptist, back from the dead. Others say Elijah; and still others, Jeremiah or one of the prophets."

"But what about you? Who do *you* say I am?"

Without hesitating, Simon proclaimed, "You are the Messiah, the Son of the living G-d."

"Blessed are you, Simon son of John, for this was not revealed to you by a human being, but by my Father in heaven. And I tell you that you are Cephas—a 'rock'—and on this rock, I will build my community." He turned to look at the cave, drawing the eyes of his disciples with him. "And I tell you that the gates of the underworld won't be able to stand against it. I'll give you the keys of the kingdom of heaven. Anything you bind on earth will be bound in heaven. Anything you loosen on earth will be loosened in heaven."

As the disciples regarded the gates of Hades, Simon's confession of Jesus as Messiah, or Son of G-d, seemed more pointed—sitting, as they were, across from statues of other human beings who had been given similar titles. Then Jesus warned his disciples not to tell anyone that he was the Messiah.

After a moment of silence, Jesus turned back to them and began explaining that he must go to Yerushalayim and suffer many things at the hands of the elders, chief priests, and teachers of the law. Indeed, that he must be killed and, on the third day, be raised to life.

Then Peter took Jesus aside and began to—in his mind—correct him. "G-d forbid, Lord! This won't happen to you." But Jesus turned to Peter and said, "Get behind me, Satan. You are a stone that could make me stumble, for you are not thinking G-d's thoughts, but human thoughts."

Then Jesus said to his disciples, "All who want to come after me must say 'no' to themselves, take up their cross, and follow me. All who want to save their lives will lose them. But all who lose their lives because of me will find them. Why would people gain the whole world but lose their lives? What will people give in exchange for their lives? For the Son of Man is going to come in his Father's glory with his angels, and then he will reward each person according to what that person has done. Amen, I say to you, some who are standing here will not taste death before they see the Son of Man coming in his dominion. Now arise, and let us leave this place."

As Jesus took them out of the northern gate, it was clear that they were not heading back to the Galilee anytime soon. As they left the city, just ahead on the horizon loomed Mount Hermon, the highest mountain in the region. But the disciples hardly noticed the view, because they were still in shock about what Jesus had said. Jesus' talk of his death—his apparently willing martyrdom—had shaken them all badly. And what was that about resurrection soon thereafter? *Was* he the Messiah? It just didn't make sense. They all believed in the resurrection of the righteous, but that would be on the Last Day, and it would include all of the righteous dead. What was Jesus talking about?

After these past several days of traveling, and now their whispered discussion about what had just been revealed to them of Jesus' identity and future mission in Israel, the disciples could see why Jesus might have decided to leave the Holy Land for a period of time. Here, they were far away from prying eyes, far from the scrutiny of the Jewish authorities. But where in the world was he going now? The answer to their question became clear when they realized they had arrived at the base of Mount Hermon, and Jesus told them to set up camp. As they unrolled their sleeping mats and gathered wood for a cooking fire, Jesus told them that he was going to take Simon, James, and John up the mountain with him.

It was a long journey, and the three disciples, who at the beginning had followed Jesus and talked among themselves, withdrew into silence after two hours of climbing, just to save breath. Again, where in the world was Jesus going? When they looked up, they could see blue sky and the sun blazing overhead, but also some low-hanging clouds.

The climbers, sweating and tired, finally emerged onto some kind of plateau. They were so high on this side of the mountain that a mist enveloped them. Looking up to get their bearings and to make sure they wouldn't lose Jesus in the mist, they saw an incredible light piercing the clouds. Then, suddenly, Jesus was transfigured before them. His clothes became dazzling white, whiter than anyone in the world could bleach them. And just as suddenly, there appeared before them two ancient-looking men, who were talking with Jesus. Being just able to hear the conversation—which was something about Jesus' leaving—his "exodus"—they looked at each other in amazement: Could this be Moses? And surely the other figure was Elijah, who himself had disappeared into the clouds on a mountain and went to Paradise. Now here they both were, talking with Jesus!

Unable to restrain himself, Cephas interrupted the conversation. The Feast of Tabernacles was still relatively fresh in his memory, and he blurted out, "Teacher, it is good for us to be here. Let us put up three shelters, one for you, one for Moses, and one for Elijah."

While Cephas was saying this, an even denser cloud appeared and enveloped them, and a voice came from the cloud, saying to the three disciples, "This is my Son, whom I love. Listen to him!" James then remembered that this was exactly what Jesus told them the heavenly voice had spoken when John baptized him. This was further confirmation of the truth of what Simon—now Cephas—had declared at Caesarea Philippi. But just as quickly as the cloud came, it disappeared, and when they looked around, they no longer saw anyone with them except Jesus.

As they were coming down the mountain, Cephas suggested that they tell the rest of the disciples about their experience, but

Jesus responded, giving them strict orders not to tell anyone what they had seen until the Son of Man had risen from the dead. So they kept the matter to themselves, still unclear what "risen from the dead" meant. What continued to confuse them was the idea that the Son of Man might rise alone, all by himself. But then they also remembered the son of the widow in Nain, and the miraculous events of that day. These were riddles within riddles.

Eager to return the conversation to more familiar ground, they asked Jesus, "Why do the teachers of the law say that Elijah must come first, and then the Messiah?"

Jesus sighed and reiterated something he had suggested before. "To be sure, Elijah does come first, and restores all things. But I tell you, Elijah has come, and they have done to him everything they wished, just as it is written about him."

Thinking that Jesus must be referring to John the Baptizer, Cephas asked, "But if that is true, then why is it necessary also that the Son of Man suffer and be killed?" But Jesus did not answer this question, and his continued silence left the three to their own thoughts as they finished descending the mountain. Somehow they knew this must be significant to the ministry of Jesus, but the events that he claimed were ahead did not seem much like "good news" to them. They yearned to return to Kefer Nahum once more, but they suspected that they would not find the peace and quiet they hoped for there.

Leaving Mount Hermon, they collected the other disciples at their base camp and headed south, eventually crossing back into Galilee. Jesus instructed the disciples not to tell anyone where they were, because he wanted some uninterrupted time to teach them. He told them once more, "The Son of Man is going to be betrayed into the hands of men. They will kill him, and after three days he will rise." His disciples still didn't understand what he meant and were afraid to ask him about it. But they kept talking to one another as Jesus went ahead, and some began to question why Jesus had picked those three to go up the mountain with him. What made them special? "Why not me?" a few asked sullenly.

In due course they arrived in Kefer Nahum. When they entered the house of Cephas' mother-in-law, Jesus asked them, "What were you arguing about on the road?" But they kept quiet, because they had argued about who was the greatest among them.

Sitting down, Jesus called the Twelve and said, "If anyone wants to be first, he must be the very last, and the servant of all." Jesus turned his attention to a little child in the house, one of Cephas' children, and he asked the boy to stand among them. Then, taking the boy in his arms, he turned to the disciples and said, "Whoever welcomes one of these little children in my name, welcomes me; and whoever welcomes me, does not welcome me but the One who sent me." And so the day ended on a familial note, setting everyone at ease, and allowing them all to sleep peacefully.

22

Sent Out on Mission

JESUS' PUBLIC MINISTRY had gone on for well over a year and a half now, and the disciples had experienced many ups and downs, surprises and frustrations, good times and not-so-good times. Jesus said and did so many things that if every one of them were recorded, there wouldn't have been enough papyrus for it all. None of the disciples could have anticipated all that they had already seen and heard. To say things had not gone as one might expect when following a teacher, would be a gross understatement. As John told them, they simply had to "roll with the punches," not knowing what would come next—a blessing or a blow.

Jesus, however, knew that time was fleeting, so he decided it was the right moment to send the disciples out. They would extend his ministry themselves, and get some experience going forward. So he gathered the Twelve, and others among his followers, and offered them one more lesson before he commissioned them and sent them out.

The disciples were sitting in a circle around Jesus on the hill above Kefer Nahum, with the crowds gathering around them as usual. He looked with affection upon them before he stood and gave them authority to drive out unclean spirits and to heal every disease and sickness. Then Jesus sent out the Twelve with the following instructions: "Don't go among the Gentiles or into a Samaritan city. Go instead to the lost sheep, the people of Israel. As you go, make this announcement, 'The dominion of heaven has come near.' Heal the sick, raise the dead, cleanse those with skin diseases, and throw out demons. You received without having to pay; therefore, give without demanding payment. Don't get gold or silver or copper coins for your money belts to take on your trips, or a backpack for the road, or two shirts or sandals or a walking stick. Remember that workers deserve to be fed.

"Whatever city or village you go into, find somebody in it who is worthy and stay there until you go on your way. When you go into a house, say, 'Peace!' If the house is worthy, give it your blessing of peace. But if the house isn't worthy, take back your blessing. If anyone refuses to welcome you or listen to your words, shake the dust off your feet as you leave that house or city. I assure you that it will be more bearable for the land of Sodom and Gomorrah on Judgment Day than it will be for that city."

He saw questioning looks pass among the disciples, and then he continued. "Look, I'm sending you as sheep among wolves. Therefore, be wise as snakes and innocent as doves. Watch out for people, because they will hand you over to councils and they will beat you in their synagogues. They will haul you in front of governors and even kings because of me, so that you may give your testimony to them and to the Gentiles. Whenever they hand you over, don't worry about how to speak or what you will say, because what you need to say will be given to you at that moment. You aren't doing the talking, but the Spirit of my Father will do the talking through you."

Jesus paused, shaking his head as a profound sadness swept over him.

"Brothers and sisters will hand each other over to be executed. A father will turn his child in. Children will defy their parents and have them executed. Everyone will hate you on account of my name. But whoever stands firm until the end will be saved. Whenever they harass you in one city, escape to the next, because I assure that you will not go through all the cities of Israel before the Son of Man comes.

"Disciples aren't greater than their teacher, and slaves aren't greater than their master. It's enough for disciples to be like their teacher and slaves like their master. If they have called the head of the house 'Beelzebub,' it's certain that they will call the members of his household by even worse names. Therefore, don't be afraid of those people, because nothing is hidden that won't be revealed, and nothing is secret that won't be brought out into the open. What I say to you in the darkness, tell in the light; and what you hear whispered, announce from the rooftops. Don't be afraid of those who can kill the body, but can't kill the spirit. Instead, be afraid of the one who can destroy both body and spirit in Gehenna. Aren't two sparrows sold for a small coin? But not one of them will fall to the ground without your Father knowing about it already. Even the hairs of your head are all counted. Don't be afraid. You are worth more than many sparrows.

"Therefore, everyone who acknowledges me before people, I also will acknowledge before my Father who is in heaven. But everyone who denies me before people, I also will deny before my Father who is in heaven. Those who love father or mother more than me aren't worthy of me. Those who love son or daughter more than me aren't worthy of me. Those who don't pick up their crosses and follow me aren't worthy of me. Those who find their lives will lose them, and those who lose their lives because of me will find them.

"Those who receive you are also receiving me, and those who receive me are receiving the One who sent me. Those who receive a prophet as a prophet will receive a prophet's reward. Those who receive a righteous person as a righteous person will receive a righteous person's reward. I assure you that everybody who gives even a cup of cold water to these little ones because they are my disciples, amen, I say to you, he will certainly not lose his reward."

Having authorized, empowered, and instructed them in this fashion, Jesus sent them out two by two, according to the word of Torah that the truth of anything must be confirmed by the testimony of two witnesses. He sent them out as his agents, extensions of his own ministry, empowered to do exactly the same things that he had already been doing, only doing them in his name, by his authority and power.

There were others present who wanted to be Jesus' disciples, and had been inspired by Jesus' challenging words on this occasion. One such person, a teacher of the Law, came to him and said, "Teacher, I will follow you wherever you go."

"Foxes have dens," replied Jesus, "and the birds in the sky have nests, but the Son of Man has no place to lay his head."

Another man who wanted to be a disciple said to him, "Lord, first let me go and bury my father."

"Follow me!" Jesus answered. "Let the dead bury their own dead."

This reply scandalized many of those present, for each of them took the instruction to honor one's parents as one of the chief commandments, and burying a parent was seen as an essential part of fulfilling that commandment. Then Jesus said to both the disciples and the crowd, "Amen, I say to you, if anyone would be my disciple, they must take up their own crosses, daily, and come and follow me."

With this stern challenge, various members of the crowd began to leave to go back to their homes, while the Twelve set out on their mission. But a large number of disciples remained to hear more from Jesus, wishing for a commission of their own. So Jesus set aside six dozen more pairs of disciples, men paired with men and women paired with women, and sent them out with the same commission, authority, and power as the Twelve. The disciples believed that Jesus was making an all-out effort to spread the good news about the in-breaking dominion of G-d throughout Galilee.

Having sent his disciples away, Jesus himself headed for the road beside the Kinneret which led south to Judaea. He had not gone far south of Tiberias, however, when a man stopped him along the way with an invitation. "Master, will you come and dine in the house of my master, Simon? He would like to make the acquaintance of a fellow teacher of Torah." It was already late in the afternoon, and Jesus was hungry, so he readily agreed to this offer.

Simon was a Pharisee who lived by the Kinneret and had heard much about Jesus—both his teaching and healing. In fact, there had been women in his little village that Jesus had healed. He wanted to meet the man his neighbors spoke about so highly. But some of his fellow Pharisees had spoken out against this teacher from the Galilee, and so he knew he needed to tread carefully. When his servant brought Jesus into his home, Simon did not rise to greet him, but instead indicated that Jesus should recline at the table, across from him. Jesus, at first confused by this lack of basic hospitality, soon realized what Simon was up to, and took his place with a wry smile.

The meal itself was simple, but excellently prepared. As it was nearing its conclusion, a woman who had lived a sinful life in that town unexpectedly and boldly entered the Pharisee's house. This woman had learned that Jesus was eating there. She came directly into the house without knocking on the door or waiting to be invited in. She brought perfumed oil in a vase made of alabaster. Standing behind Jesus at his feet and crying, she knelt and began to wet his feet with her tears. She wiped them with her hair, kissed them, and poured the oil on them. When the Pharisee who had invited Jesus saw what was happening, he said to himself, *If this man were a prophet, he would know what kind of woman is touching him. He would know that she is a sinner.*

Jesus responded to Simon's unspoken thought. "Simon, I have something to say to you."

Simon looked at the other guests, who were clearly as scandalized as he was, and said, "Teacher, speak."

"A certain moneylender had two debtors. One owed enough money to pay five hundred people for a day's work. The other owed enough money for fifty. When they couldn't pay, the lender forgave the debts of them both. Which of them will love him more?"

Simon replied, but somewhat hesitantly, as he was confused by the question. "I suppose the one who had the largest debt canceled."

"You have judged correctly," Jesus replied. He turned to the woman, but continued to speak to Simon.

"Do you see this woman? When I entered here, you did not fulfill your responsibilities to me as a guest in your home. You gave me no water to wash the dust of the road from my feet, but she has wet my feet with tears and wiped them with her hair. You didn't greet me with a kiss, but she hasn't stopped kissing my feet since I came in. You didn't anoint my head with oil, but she has poured perfumed oil on my feet. This is why I say to you now that because her many sins have been forgiven, she has shown great love. But the one who is forgiven little, loves little."

Then Jesus said to her, "Your sins *are* forgiven."

The other guests at the table began to say among themselves, "Who is this person that even forgives sins? No one can forgive sin but G-d alone."

Jesus smiled at them as if to say, "You have said it!" Then he turned to the woman and said to her, "Your faith has saved you; go in the shalom of G-d." With that, Jesus thanked Simon for the meal, excused himself, and left—shortly after the woman had departed, her head held high.

23

Upside-Down Stories

TRAVELING ALONE AS he was, the journey to Yerushalayim this time had been somewhat quiet and uneventful. But as Jesus walked along the border between Samaria and Galilee, the peace he had been enjoying came to an abrupt end. He entered a village where ten men with various skin diseases approached him. But they still kept a certain distance, and raised their voices and cried out, "Jesus, Master, show us mercy!"

When Jesus saw them, he said, "Go, show yourselves to the priests." The men left, but looking around at each other, they discovered that they had been cleansed. One of them, when he saw this, returned and praised G-d with a loud voice. He fell on his face at Jesus' feet and thanked him. The man was a Samaritan. Jesus replied, "Weren't ten cleansed? Where are the other nine? No one returned to praise G-d except this foreigner?"

Then Jesus said to the man, "Get up and go. Your faith has healed you." Shaking his head after this episode, Jesus murmured to himself, "Some will come from unexpected places and sit at the messianic banquet, even taking places once reserved for G-d's chosen people."

As he approached Bet Anya, Jesus realized just how much he had been looking forward to another visit with Lazarus, Martha, and Mary. With winter already upon them, it was the season to celebrate Hanukkah, the Feast of Lights, and Jesus was determined to teach in the temple. But first he would spend time with his friends. He had much to share with these dear ones who seemed to understand his vision of the future.

After Lazarus greeted him with a bear hug, Jesus spent his first evening in Bet Anya catching up on the lives of his friends and sharing with them what had been happening to him. Lazarus proposed having a big banquet in Jesus' honor, and inviting people he knew were sympathetic to his teaching. Like many others, Lazarus wanted to know more about the message Jesus had proclaimed in Galilee, since he had heard the teaching there was somewhat different than the things Jesus said in Judaea. He was especially keen to hear some of the many parables. Jesus readily agreed to this proposition, and a couple of nights later, he found himself offering words for reflection and response, as was the custom when all were reclining and drinking a little wine after their meal.

"Let me begin by telling you three stories about the lost, and how Abba seeks them out," he began. "Suppose someone among you had a hundred sheep and lost one of them. Wouldn't he leave the other ninety-nine in the pasture and search for the lost one until he finds it? And when he finds it, he is thrilled and places it on his shoulders. When he arrives home, he calls together his friends and neighbors, saying to them, 'Celebrate with me, because I've found my lost sheep.' In the same way, I tell you, there will be more joy in heaven over one sinner who changes both heart and life than over ninety-nine righteous people who have no need to change their hearts and lives."

One of the listeners interrupted at this point and said, "But a shepherd would not normally leave his whole flock to go and rescue one sheep, would he?"

Jesus replied, "G-d's ways are not always like ours."

He told a second parable in the same vein. "What woman, if she owns ten silver coins and loses one of them, won't light a lamp and sweep the house, searching her home carefully until she finds it? When she finds it, she calls together her friends and neighbors, saying, 'Celebrate with me because I've found my lost coin.' In the same way, I tell you, joy breaks out in the presence of G-d's angels over one sinner who changes both heart and life."

Jesus looked around at the group before telling a third story. "A certain man had two sons. The younger son said to his father, 'Father, give me my share of the inheritance.'"

There was a collective gasp in the room over such scandalous words. What a terrible thing, for the young man was in effect saying he wished his father was dead! But Jesus' description of the father's response seemed even more outrageous. "Then the father divided his estate between them. Soon afterward, the younger son gathered everything together and took a trip to a land far away. There, he wasted his wealth through extravagant living." Those listening shook their heads in distaste. Where was this story heading?

"When the son had used up his resources, a severe food shortage arose in that country and he began to be in need. He hired himself out to a man who sent him into the fields to feed pigs. He was so hungry and desperate that he would have gladly eaten his fill from what the pigs ate, but no one gave him anything."

"And rightfully so," a guest murmured under his breath.

Jesus continued. "When the son came to his senses, he said, 'How many of my father's hired hands have more than enough food, but here I am, starving to death! I will get up and go to my father, and say to him, "Father, I have sinned against heaven and against you. I no longer deserve to be called your son. Take me on as one of your hired hands."' And so he went home to his father."

Jesus took a sip of wine, allowing the tension of the story to be heightened during the pause. "While the son was still a long way off, his father saw him and was moved with compassion. The old man ran to him, hugged him, and kissed him. Then his son said, 'Father, I have sinned against heaven and against you. I no longer deserve to be called your son.' But the father said to his servants, 'Quickly, bring out the best robe and put it on him! Put a ring on his finger and sandals on his feet! Fetch the fattened calf and slaughter it. We must celebrate with feasting, because this son of mine was dead and has come back to life! He was lost and is found!' And they began to celebrate."

The murmuring was much louder now. What kind of parable was this?

"Now the man's older son was in the field. Coming in from his work, he approached the house and heard music and dancing. He called one of the servants and asked what was going on. The servant replied, 'Your brother came home, and your father has slaughtered the fattened calf because he has received his son back safe and sound.' Then the older son was furious and refused to enter the house, but his father came out and begged him to join the celebration.

"The older son answered, 'Look, I've served you all these years, and I have never failed to obey even one of your instructions. Yet you've never given me as much as a young goat so I could celebrate with my friends. But when he returned, after squandering his inheritance on prostitutes, you slaughtered the fattened calf for him.' Then his father said, 'Son, you are always with me, and everything I have is yours. But we *must* celebrate and be glad because this brother of yours was dead and is now alive. He was lost and is found.'"

Silence greeted the end of this parable, with many of the guests shaking their heads. Lazarus broke the silence. "Master, these stories seem to explain why you've been reaching out to sinners and tax collectors and the like. G-d wishes to save everyone, all the lost sheep of Israel." But some in the gathering took exception to what Jesus was saying. Realizing this, he told another parable for the sake of those who had convinced themselves that they were righteous and who looked on others with contempt.

"Two people went up to the temple to pray. One was a Pharisee and the other a tax collector. The Pharisee stood and prayed about himself with these words, 'G-d, I thank you that I'm not like everyone else—crooks, evildoers, adulterers, or even like this tax collector. I fast twice a week. I give a tenth of everything I receive.' But the tax collector stood at a distance. In humility, he couldn't even bring himself to lift his eyes to look toward heaven. Rather, he struck his chest and said, 'G-d, show mercy to me, a sinner.'" Jesus fixed an almost stern gaze on the dinner guests. "I tell you, this is the person who went back to his home justified, and not the Pharisee. All who lift themselves up will be brought low, and those who make themselves low will be lifted up."

Now the silence was even more uncomfortable. It was finally broken by a man who clearly wished to change the subject. "Teacher, tell us something of your message about future things.

What happens to a righteous man when he dies? And when and where will our reward be granted?"

"Let those who have two good ears listen to this parable," replied Jesus. "There was a certain rich man who clothed himself in purple and fine linen, and who feasted luxuriously every day. At his gate lay a certain poor man named Lazarus, who was covered with sores."

With this, Lazarus interrupted. "This parable sounds strangely familiar."

Jesus smiled, winked at his host, and then continued. "Now this *other* Lazarus longed to eat the crumbs that fell from the rich man's table. Instead, dogs would come and lick his sores. The poor man died and was carried by angels to Abraham's side. The rich man also died and was buried. While being tormented in Gehenna, he looked up and saw Abraham at a distance with Lazarus at his side. He shouted, 'Father Abraham, have mercy on me. Send Lazarus to dip the tip of his finger in water and cool my tongue, because I'm suffering in this flame.' But Abraham said, 'Child, remember that during your lifetime you received good things, whereas Lazarus received terrible things. Now Lazarus is being comforted and you are in great pain. Moreover, a great chasm has been fixed between us and you. Those who wish to cross over from here to you cannot. Neither can anyone cross from there to us.'

"The rich man said, 'Then I beg you, father, send Lazarus to my father's house. I have five brothers. He needs to warn them, so that they don't come to this place of agony.' Abraham replied, 'They have Moses and the prophets. They must listen to them.' The rich man said, 'No, Father Abraham! But if someone from the dead goes to them, they will change their hearts and lives.'

Abraham said, 'If they don't listen to Moses and the prophets, then neither will they be persuaded if someone rises from the dead.'" With these words, Jesus suddenly bowed his head.

This parable immediately struck a chord in Lazarus' own heart, since his father had died of leprosy and the man in question was named Lazarus. But on the other hand, he had never been a poor beggar, so Jesus was surely not talking about him. Martha spoke up and said, "So you're saying that in the afterlife, justice will be done. But will it not also be done in the end of days here on earth as well? Will we never see justice triumph here in Yerushalayim?"

"Yes, you will, on that day when the Son of Man returns," replied Jesus. Realizing he had given them enough to think about for one evening, and when there was no further response, Jesus offered a blessing and Lazarus dismissed the guests. As they were clearing the table, Lazarus said to Jesus, "You realize that opposition to you here in Yerushalayim has been building since your last visit. Are you sure you want to go and teach in the temple precincts in the morning?"

Jesus held his friend's shoulders and looked into his eyes. "The night is coming when I will no longer be able to do my work. I must seize the day while there is still light." He pulled Lazarus into a brief hug before saying, "Good night, my friend." Lazarus watched Jesus walk across the courtyard to the guest room, and thought he saw Jesus' shoulders sink as he walked through the doorway.

24

Confrontation in the Temple

LAZARUS AND THE two sisters, and several other sympathizers gathered with Jesus very early the next morning to walk with him up to Yerushalayim and into the temple courts. When word spread that he was on the way, the Jewish authorities' plan to put him to the test the next time he came sprang into effect. They hoped such an incident would cause Jesus to lose face before the crowds, and this upstart teacher would be brought into line.

The people gathered around him, and he sat down to teach. As he did so, the teachers of the Law and the Pharisees brought in a woman who had been caught in adultery.[1] They made her stand before the group and said to Jesus, "Teacher, this woman was

1. This beloved story was probably not in the earliest form of John's Gospel, but appears to be an authentic story from the life of Jesus, just a non-canonical one that later scribes inserted in three different places in the Gospel of John, and which one scribe even tried to insert into Luke's Gospel. It was an authentic text looking for a home.

caught in the very act of adultery. In the Law, Moses commanded us to stone such women. Now, what do *you* say?" They were using this question as a trap, to give them a basis for accusing him. Martha instantly saw through their ruse, and dug her elbow into her sister's ribs, saying—loudly enough to be heard—"Where's the man?!" She looked accusingly at the elders, who clearly had not dealt fairly with this woman. They had not accused or brought forward the woman's partner, and it was they who were tasked with being the moral guides of the community, responsible to make sure the Law was implemented fairly and with mercy for all.

Jesus bent down and started to write on the ground with his finger. They persisted in questioning him, and he at last stood up and said, "If any one of you is without sin, let him be the first to throw a stone at her." Again he stooped down and wrote on the ground. At this, those who heard began to walk away one at a time, the older ones first, until only Jesus was left with the woman.

She was visibly shaken and still standing in the same spot, her eyes firmly fixed on the ground. Jesus stood again and asked her, "Woman, where are they? Has no one condemned you?"

She lifted her eyes, and only then saw that everyone had left. With a note of wonder in her voice she said, "No one, sir."

"Then neither do I condemn you," Jesus declared. "Go now and leave your life of sin behind."

As he watched the woman cross the vast courtyard, Jesus felt his anger rise once more at the lack of compassion the "shepherds" of Israel displayed for those in their care. He walked to an area of the temple known as the treasury and sat down. A crowd slowly reconvened around him, including some Pharisees, intent on monitoring his every word.

Jesus stood up to address the crowd. "I am the light of the world. Whoever follows me won't walk in darkness, but will have the light of life."

This was too much for the Pharisees, who challenged him, saying, "Because you are testifying about yourself, your testimony isn't valid."

Jesus answered them, saying, "Even if I testify about myself, my testimony is true, since I know where I came from and where I'm going. You have no idea where I come from or where I'm going. You judge according to human standards, but I judge no one. Even if I do judge, my judgment is truthful, because I'm not alone. My judgments come from me and from the Father who sent me. In your Law it is written that the witness of two people is true. I am one witness concerning myself, and the Father who sent me is the other."

"Where is your Father?" one Pharisee asked with a sneer.

"You don't know me, and you don't know my Father. If you knew me, you would also know my Father." It was clear to everyone present that the Pharisees were seething with rage at Jesus' words. But no one arrested him, because his time had not yet come.

Jesus continued, "I'm going away. You will look for me, and you will die in your sin. Where I'm going, you can't come."

Some of the Jewish officials present turned to each other and whispered, "He isn't going to kill himself, is he? Is that why he said, 'Where I'm going, you can't come'?"

Jesus said to them, "You are from below; I'm from above. You are from this world; I am not from this world. This is why I told you that you would die in your sins. If you don't believe that I Am, you will die in your sins."

"Who are you?"

"I'm exactly who I have claimed to be from the beginning. I have many things to say in judgment concerning you. The One who sent me is true, and what I have heard from him I tell the world." They didn't know that he was speaking about his Father. So Jesus said to them, "When you lift up the Son of Man, then you will know that I Am, and that I do nothing on my own initiative, but I say just what the Father has taught me. He who sent me is with me. He doesn't leave me by myself, because I always do what pleases him." As he spoke, many people began to put their faith in him.

Jesus said to those who had believed in him, "You are truly my disciples if you remain faithful to my teaching. Then you will know the truth, and the truth will set you free."

Some called out, "We are Abraham's children; we've never been anyone's slaves. How can you say that we will be set free?"

"I assure you that everyone who sins is a slave to sin. A slave isn't a permanent member of the household, but a son is. Therefore, if the Son makes you free, you really will be free. I know that you are Abraham's children, yet you want to kill me because you don't welcome my teaching. I'm telling you what I've seen when I am with the Father, but you are doing what you've heard from your father."

They retorted, "Our father is Abraham."

"If you actually were Abraham's children, you would do Abraham's works. Instead, you want to kill me, though I am the One who has spoken the truth I heard from G-d. Abraham didn't do this. You are doing your father's works."

"Our ancestry isn't in question! We are not illegitimate children! The only Father we have is G-d!"

"If G-d were your Father, you would love me, for I came from G-d. Here I am. I haven't come on my own. G-d sent me. Why don't you understand what I'm saying? It's because you can't really hear my words. Your father is the devil. You are his children, and you want to do what your father wants. He was a murderer from the beginning. He has never stood for the truth, because there's no truth in him. Whenever that liar speaks, he speaks according to his own nature, because he's a liar and the father of liars. Because I speak the truth, you don't believe me. Who among you can show I'm guilty of sin? Since I speak the truth, why don't you believe me? G-d's children listen to G-d's words. You don't listen to me because you aren't G-d's children."

Some of the Jewish authorities who had heard that Jesus spent time in Samaria and had converts there called out, "We were right to say that you are a Samaritan and have a demon, weren't we?"

"I don't have a demon," Jesus replied. "But I honor my Father and you dishonor me. I'm not trying to bring glory to myself. There is one who is seeking to glorify me, and he is the judge. Amen, amen, I assure you, if anyone keeps my word, he will never see death."

At this the Jewish officials exclaimed, "Now we know that you have a demon. Abraham and the prophets died, yet you say, 'Whoever keeps my word will never die.' Are you greater than our father Abraham? He died and the prophets died, so who do you make yourself out to be?"

"If I glorify myself, my glory is meaningless. My Father, who you say is your G-d, is the One who glorifies me. You don't know him, but I do. If I said I didn't know him, I would be like you, a liar. But I do know him, and I keep his word. Your father

Abraham was overjoyed that he would see my day. He saw it and was happy."

"You aren't even fifty years old! How can you say that you have seen Abraham?"

"I assure you, before Abraham was born, I Am." Many of the crowd gasped at this seemingly blasphemous remark, and some even picked up stones to stone him. But Jesus slipped through the crowd and away from the temple grounds. Saying a brief good-bye to Lazarus, Martha, and Mary, he embraced his friends before slipping out of town, heading once more toward Jericho and the road that would lead back to Galilee. The situation was intensifying, and Jesus knew he had to make the most of the time he had left.

25

A Storm at Sea

WHEN JESUS REUNITED with the disciples, he found them posi-
tively excited about their experiences since he had sent them out,
but at the same time a little perplexed. On the one hand, they
had been received with appreciation in many places. And yet,
it appeared that all sorts of people were now attempting healings and exorcisms in Jesus' name. "Teacher," said John, son of
Zebedee, "we saw a man driving out demons in your name and we
told him to stop, because he wasn't following us."

"Don't stop him!" Jesus replied. "No one who does powerful
acts in my name can quickly turn around and curse me. Whoever
is not against us is for us. I assure you that whoever gives you
a cup of water to drink because you belong to the Messiah will
certainly be rewarded.

"As for whoever causes these little ones who believe in me to
stumble and fall into sin, it would be better for that person to
have a huge millstone hung around their neck and to be thrown
into the lake. If your hand causes you to fall into sin, chop it off.
It's better for you to enter into life crippled than to go away with
two hands in the fire of Gehenna, which can't be put out. If your

foot causes you to fall into sin, chop it off. It's better for you to enter life lame than to be thrown into Gehenna with two feet. If your eye causes you to fall into sin, tear it out. It's better for you to enter G-d's dominion with one eye than to be thrown into Gehenna with two. That's a place where worms don't die and the fire never goes out. Everyone will be salted with fire. Salt is good; but if salt loses its saltiness, how will it become salty again? Maintain salt in yourselves, and be at peace with one another."

It appeared that the disciples had fulfilled the mission he sent them on, and Jesus decided to extend their apprenticeship in the work of G-d's dominion. He led them down to the Kinneret, where they got in a boat and headed south, intending to disembark and follow the east bank of the Jordan River.

As they readied the boat, Peter looked somewhat nervously at the clouds forming overhead. It was a chilly winter day, a season known for storms, but this did not seem to deter Jesus as he told his disciples to weigh anchor and head across the lake. The Kinneret is a bowl-shaped lake sitting among hills and winds can come up quickly and create choppy waves, almost without warning.

Leaving the crowd behind, they headed down the lake, accompanied by some other boats. Suddenly a furious squall came up, and the waves broke over the boat, so that it was nearly swamped. The boat pitched and rolled, and it seemed to the disciples it was likely to sink. As seasoned fishermen, they knew enough to be afraid. But where was Jesus? Huddled under a low shelf in the stern, reclining on a cushion and fast asleep. The disciples, becoming frantic, woke him and asked, "Teacher, don't you care if we drown?"

Jesus got up, assessed the situation, and rebuked the wind, saying to the waves, "Quiet! Be still!" Suddenly, the wind died down and it was completely calm. What most stunned the disciples, even the fishermen among them, was that while the wind could come and go quickly, once the water was stirred up, it remained choppy for a good period of time. But not this time. Jesus had stopped both wind and wave instantly. Jesus looked at them and saw the fear in their eyes, fear caused not just by the storm but by what Jesus had just done. He pressed them, asking, "Why are you so afraid? Do you still have no faith?"

In truth, it *was* beginning to dawn on them that Jesus was no ordinary, mortal man. But he clearly was also not the Messiah that they expected. In their terror they asked each other, "Who is this? Even the wind and the waves obey him!" Who, indeed?

Having reached the southern shore of the lake, they disembarked and set off. The journey down the familiar north-south road was uneventful, not least because few people traveled any distance at this time of year. Jesus had hoped to go to the spot where he had been baptized, returning to where his ministry had really begun. Perhaps not many would be expecting him there, and he would have time to further prepare his disciples for what was to come. It was raining as they walked along, so they pulled their outer garments up over their heads. They believed that no one would recognize them in these conditions. But, in fact, the word had already spread that Jesus was entering Judaea once more, and large crowds were on the lookout. When they spotted him, they followed him, and he healed many of them there.

After a day or so, some Pharisees came down from Yerushalayim to test Jesus yet again. They asked, "Is it lawful for a man to divorce his wife for any reason at all?"

Jesus sighed deeply. "Haven't you read that at the beginning the Creator made them male and female? And G-d said, 'For this reason a man shall leave his father and mother and be joined together with his wife, and the two will be one flesh.' So they are no longer two but one. Therefore, humans shouldn't pull apart what G-d has put together."

The Pharisees jumped on Jesus' response. "Then why did Moses command us to give a divorce certificate and divorce her?"

"Moses did not *command* divorce, he *allowed* you to divorce your wives because your hearts are hard. But it wasn't that way from the beginning. I say to you that whoever divorces his wife, except for incest, and marries another woman, commits adultery."

It was clear to the disciples that Jesus was essentially taking away the male privilege of divorce. One suggested to him, "If that's the way things are between a man and his wife, then is it better not to marry?"

Jesus replied, "Not everybody can accept this teaching, but only those who have received the ability to accept it. For there are eunuchs who have been eunuchs from birth. And there are eunuchs who have been made eunuchs by other people. And then there are eunuchs who have made themselves eunuchs because of the dominion of heaven. Those who can accept it should accept it."

"I certainly can't accept it," said Peter, to much laughter. Jesus shook his head with an affectionate smile.

Some women approached them, with their children in tow. Often women had brought their little children to Jesus in the hope that he would bless them. Tenderly, carefully, Jesus would lay his hands on them and pray for them. But with their dawning realization of who Jesus was, the disciples began to rebuke those women who now brought their children to Jesus. Many believed that small children had no place in meetings where a teacher was instructing adults, let alone a teacher who just may be the Messiah. But Jesus rebuked his disciples in turn, saying, "Let the little children come to me, and do not hinder them, for the dominion of heaven belongs to such as these." After he had placed his hands on them all, he went on from there, managing to get away from the crowds for the moment.

Jesus knew what lay ahead of him, and after much prayer and reflection, he set his face like flint to journey to Yerushalayim. When he announced this to the men and women who formed the core group among his disciples, they were astonished. Others who followed became afraid. Again he took the Twelve aside and told them what was going to happen to him. "We are going up to Yerushalayim, and the Son of Man will be betrayed to the chief priests and teachers of the Law. They will condemn him to death and will hand him over to the Gentiles, who will mock him and spit on him, flog him, and kill him. Three days later he will rise."

As a heaviness fell over the group, James and John, the sons of Zebedee, came to Jesus and, as if they had not heard a word he had just spoken, said, "Teacher, we want you to do for us whatever we ask."

"What do you want me to do for you?"

"Let one of us sit at your right and the other at your left when you come into your glory."

"You don't know what you are asking. Can you drink the cup I drink or be baptized with the baptism with which I am baptized?"

"We certainly can," they answered with the naiveté and assurance of young men, especially young men who had performed miracles, and who now believed that all kinds of things were possible for them.

Jesus regarded them with a heavy heart. "You will indeed drink the cup I drink and be baptized with the baptism I am baptized with, but to sit at my right or left is not for me to grant. These places belong to those for whom they have been prepared."

When the other ten heard their request, they became indignant with James and John. Jesus called them all together and said, "You know that those who are regarded as rulers of the Gentiles lord it over them, and their high officials exercise authority over them. It is not to be so with you. Instead, whoever wants to become great among you must be your servant, and whoever wants to be first must be slave of all. For even the Son of Man did not come to be served, but to serve, and to give his life as a ransom for many.

"Amen, I say to you, at the renewal of all things, when the Son of Man sits on his glorious throne, you who have followed me will also sit on twelve thrones, judging the twelve tribes of Israel. And everyone who has left houses or brothers or sisters or father or mother or children or fields for my sake will receive a hundred times as much and will inherit everlasting life. But many who are first will be last, and many who are last will be first."

The disciples looked at each other. Who were they anyway? Fishermen? Tax collectors? They were merely ordinary men from various walks of life, lowly backgrounds, and sinners like everyone else. Why had they been chosen by Jesus in the first place? Surely it was just an act of G-d's pure grace. And just as surely, the end must be at hand, for the blind were receiving their sight, the demons were being cast out, and the dead were being raised to life.

But as for Jesus himself, he was beginning to realize that when you empty yourself, and take on the form of a servant or slave, you are likely to end up with the fate of a servant or slave: death by crucifixion, the punishment for runaway and rebellious slaves. And no one thought *that* was a noble martyr's way to die—no one.

26

The Blind Leading the Blind

JESUS AND THE disciples came to Jericho, the city that another man named Yeshua[1] had made famous in ancient times. It had gained more recent prominence as the site of Herod the Great's summer palace, and various priests and Levites made their home there because it was so close to Yerushalayim. Herod had, in fact, died painfully in Jericho.

It was also a border town, so various toll and tax collectors resided there as well. One of these men, Zacchaeus, had bid successfully for the job of overseeing Roman tax collections in Jericho, and as a result he was very wealthy. He had long been curious about Jesus, and as word spread that the teacher was passing through town, he hurried to the main street. But the crowd pushed him away because, as a tax collector, he was held in low regard by his neighbors. So he ran ahead and climbed a

---

1. "Yeshua" is the Hebrew name which we render as "Jesus," and which is rendered as "Joshua" in the book of the Bible that bears his name.

sycomore (fig tree) for a better view. When Jesus reached the tree, he looked up and saw Zacchaeus.

"Zacchaeus," he said, "come down immediately. I must stay at your house today."

Zacchaeus hurried down the tree and welcomed Jesus gladly. All of the people saw this and, taken aback by it, they began to mutter about Jesus: "He has gone to be the guest of a sinner."

Once Jesus and his disciples entered Zacchaeus' house, they reclined on couches for a time, eating and drinking and listening to Jesus' teaching. Then Zacchaeus stood up and said to Jesus, "Look, Master! Here and now I give half of my possessions to the poor, and if I have cheated anybody out of anything, I will pay back four times the amount." Jesus smiled and said to him, "Today salvation has come to this house, because this man, too, is a son of Abraham. For the Son of Man came to seek and to save what was lost."

Of all the disciples, Matthew was most pleased with this encounter and its remarkable outcome. He continued to comment on it as Jesus and his disciples, together with a large crowd, were leaving the city.

As they approached the westernmost gate of the city, they came upon a blind man named Bartimaeus—that is, the son of Timaeus—who was sitting by the roadside begging. When he heard that it was Jesus of Netzerit who approached, he began to shout out, "Jesus, Son of David, have mercy on me!"

Many rebuked him and told him to be quiet, but he shouted all the more, "Son of David, have mercy on me!" He shouted these words because it was believed that Solomon, the Son of David, had the wisdom to cure; and since Jesus seemed to have such wisdom, Bartimaeus addressed him as one like—but perhaps greater than—Solomon.

Jesus stopped and said, "Call him over." So they called to the blind man, "Cheer up! On your feet! He's calling for you." Throwing his cloak aside, Bartimaeus jumped to his feet and groped his way toward Jesus. It was heartrending to see the man slowly making his way forward by listening to the sound and direction of the voices, with hands outstretched to make sure he didn't bump into anyone by accident. Nathan'el pushed through the crowd and, gently taking his arm, led him to Jesus.

"What do you want me to do for you?" Jesus asked him in a soft voice, as though they were having a private conversation.

"Master, I desperately want to see."

"Go," said Jesus. "Your faith has healed you." Immediately Bartimaeus received his sight, but instead of heading back into town, he followed Jesus and the disciples along the road.

They continued their walk to Yerushalayim, coming into the city from the southeast over the Mount of Olives and down toward the Kidron and the Pool of Siloam. As Jesus went along, he saw another blind man, a well-known beggar who had been blind from birth. His disciples followed Jesus' gaze, and asked him, "Master, who sinned—this man or his parents—that he was born blind?"

Jesus answered, "Neither he nor his parents. This happened so that G-d might have the opportunity to do a mighty work in him. While it's daytime, we must do the works of him who sent me. Night is coming, when no one can work. While I am in the world, I am the light of the world."

After he said this, Jesus spat on the ground, made mud with the saliva, and smeared the mud on the man's eyes. This was not unusual, for it was believed that a holy man's saliva had healing properties. But Jesus was also concerned that the blind man participate in his own healing. Jesus said to him, "Go, wash in the Pool of *Siloam*"—a word that means "sent."

So the man went away and washed. When he returned, he could see. The man's neighbors and those who had seen him when he was a beggar said, "Isn't this the man who used to sit and beg?" Some said, "It is," while others said, "No, it's someone who looks like him."

But the man said, "Yes, it's me!"

So they asked him, "How are you now able to see?"

"The man they call Jesus made mud, smeared it on my eyes, and said, 'Go, wash in the Pool of Siloam.' So I went and washed, and then I could see."

"Where is this man?"

"I don't know."

Then they led the man who had been born blind to the Pharisees, who also asked how he was able to see.

He told them, "A man put mud on my eyes, I washed, and now I see."

Jesus had performed this miracle on Shabbat. Some Pharisees said, "This man isn't from G-d, because he breaks Shabbat law." Others said, "How can a sinner do miraculous signs like these?" So they were divided. Some of the Pharisees again questioned the man who had been born blind. "What do you have to say about him, since he healed your eyes?"

"He's a prophet."

No one believed that the man had been blind and received his sight until they called for his parents. The Jewish officials asked them, "Is this your son? Can you confirm that he was born blind? How is it that he can now see?"

His parents answered, "We know he is our son. We know he was born blind. But we don't know how he now sees, and we don't know who healed his eyes. Ask him. He's old enough to speak for himself." They said this because they feared the Jewish authorities, who had already decided that anyone who confessed Jesus to be the Messiah would be expelled from the synagogue.

The Pharisees then called a second time for the man who had been born blind, and said to him, "Give glory to G-d. We know this man is a sinner."

"I don't know whether he's a sinner. Here's what I do know: I was blind and now I see."

They questioned him further. "What did he do to you? How did he heal your eyes?"

He replied with some exasperation, "I have already told you, and you didn't listen. Why do you want to hear it again? Do you want to become his disciples too?"

They began to hurl insults at him. "You are his disciple, but we are *Moses'* disciples. We know that G-d spoke to Moses, but we don't know where this man is from."

The man answered, a hint of sarcasm in his voice, "This is incredible! You don't know where he is from, yet he healed my eyes! We know that G-d doesn't listen to sinners. G-d listens to anyone who is devout and does G-d's will. No one has ever heard of a healing of the eyes of someone born blind. If this man wasn't from G-d, he could do nothing."

The Pharisees were enraged. "You were born completely in sin! How is it that you dare to teach *us*?" Then they expelled him.

Jesus heard they had expelled the man born blind. Finding him, Jesus said, "Do you believe in the Son of Man?"

"Who is he, sir? I want to believe in him."

"You have seen him. In fact, he is the One speaking with you."

"Master, I believe." And he prostrated himself before Jesus.

Jesus said, "For judgment I have come into this world, so that the blind will see, and those who see will become blind." Some Pharisees who were with him heard him say this and asked incredulously, "What? Are you saying we are blind too?"

Jesus turned to them. "If you were actually blind, you would not be guilty of sin; but now that you claim you can see, your guilt remains." Jesus left them and went to Bet Anya to spend the night.

It was winter and the time for Hanukkah, the Feast of Lights. Jesus went to the temple in Yerushalayim, walking in the covered porch named for Solomon. The Jewish officials circled around him and asked, "How long will you test our patience? If you *are* the Messiah, tell us plainly."

"I have told you, but you don't believe me. The works I do in my Father's name testify about me, but you don't believe because you don't belong to my sheep. My sheep listen to my voice. I know them and they follow me. I give them eternal life. They will never die, and no one will snatch them from my hand. My Father, who has given them to me, is greater than all, and no one is able to snatch them from my Father's hand. I and the Father are one."

As had happened before, the Jewish officials picked up stones in order to stone him. Jesus responded, "I have shown you many good works from the Father. For which of those works do you stone me?"

"We don't stone you for a good work, but for insulting G-d. You are merely a man, yet you make yourself out to be G-d!"

Jesus replied, "Isn't it written in your Law, 'I have said, you are gods'? Scripture calls those to whom G-d's word came, 'gods,' and Scripture can't be abolished. So how can you say that the One whom the Father has made holy and sent into the world insults G-d, because he said, 'I am G-d's Son'? If I don't do the works of my Father, don't believe me. But if I do them, and you don't believe me, at least believe the works so that you can know and recognize that the Father is in me and I am in the Father."

Then Jesus began the doxology, lifting up his hands and saying, "I praise you, Father, Lord of heaven and earth, because you've hidden these things from the wise and intelligent and have revealed them to infants. Indeed, Father, this brings you happiness."

Turning again to the Pharisees, Jesus said, "My Father has handed all things over to me. No one knows the Son except the Father. And nobody knows the Father except the Son and anyone to whom the Son wants to reveal him."

And then, lifting his eyes beyond the Pharisees to the crowds behind them, Jesus spoke. "Come to me, all you who are struggling hard and carrying heavy loads, and I will give you rest. Put on my yoke, and learn from me. I'm gentle and humble. And you will find rest for yourselves. My yoke is easy to bear, and my burden is light."

The Pharisees tried to seize him for this latest outrage, as it seemed he was claiming to be divine and daring to speak of his own authority concerning the Law. After all, the Law was "G-d's yoke" or "Moses' yoke." It was not *Jesus'* yoke. But once again, Jesus eluded their grasp, slipped out of the temple, and left Yerushalayim.

He went back across the Jordan to the place where John the Baptizer had ministered in the early days. For a while, he and his disciples remained there in safety, and many people came to him. They said, "Though John never performed a miraculous sign, all that John said about this man was true." They believed in Jesus, in part because he had healed the blind—a miracle never recorded in the Scriptures, but only foretold in Isaiah.

The Tomb of Lazarus

WORD REACHED JESUS that Lazarus, his friend and most beloved disciple, had become gravely ill. Mary and Martha sent a messenger to tell him, "Master, the one you love is sick." When he heard this, Jesus said to his disciples, "This sickness will not end in death. No, it is for G-d's glory, so that G-d's Son may be glorified through it."

Jesus loved this family, yet when he heard that Lazarus was sick, he remained where he was two more days. Then he said to his disciples, "Let us go back to Judaea."

"But Master," they said, "a short while ago, some Judaeans tried to stone you. And yet you want to go back there?"

"Are there not twelve hours of daylight?" Jesus replied. "A man who walks by day will not stumble, for he sees by this world's light. It is when he walks by night that he stumbles, for he has no light. Our friend Lazarus has fallen asleep; I am going there to wake him up."

His disciples, increasingly alarmed by Jesus' apparent disregard for his safety, said, "Master, if he sleeps, he will get better." Jesus had been speaking of Lazarus' death, but his disciples thought he meant natural sleep. Seeing this, he told them plainly, "Lazarus is dead, and for your sake I am glad I was not there, so that you may believe. But come, let us go to him."

Then Thomas, called Didymus, or "Twin"—the most skeptical of the disciples—said to the others, "Let us also go, that we may die with him." Thomas was a fatalistic sort of fellow, and some of the other disciples wondered if he had any faith at all. They liked Thomas well enough, but sometimes they wondered why Jesus would choose a person that skeptical and pessimistic to be one of the Twelve. Yet, ironically, Thomas saw most clearly what the others were in denial about: that Jesus would indeed be going to Yerushalayim to die. And he was ready to die with him.

On his arrival in Bet Anya, Jesus found that Lazarus had already been in the tomb for four days. Bet Anya was less than two miles from Yerushalayim, and many Judaeans had come to Martha and Mary to comfort them in the loss of their brother. When Martha heard that Jesus was coming, she went out to meet him along the road into town, but Mary stayed at home.

"Lord, if you had been here, my brother wouldn't have died. But even now I know that whatever you ask G-d, Go-d will give you."

Jesus saw the desperate hope in her eyes and said, "Your brother will rise again."

Martha, not understanding what Jesus meant by this, shook her head sadly. "I *know* that he will rise in the resurrection of the righteous on the last day."

Jesus gently took her chin in one hand and lifted her eyes to his. "I am the resurrection and the life. Whoever believes in me will live, even though they die. Everyone who lives and believes in me will never die. Do you believe this?"

"Yes, Lord, I have believed that you are the long-promised Messiah, G-d's Son, the One who is coming into the world." She held Jesus' gaze for a moment, and then stepped back from his touch. They spoke briefly and then she turned, and walked quickly toward the village.

She went home and found her sister, Mary. "The teacher is here and he's calling for you." When Mary heard this, she got up quickly and went to Jesus. He hadn't entered the village but was still in the place where Martha had met him. When the Judaeans, who were comforting Mary in the house, saw her get up quickly and leave, they followed her. They assumed she was going to mourn at the tomb.

Mary arrived where Jesus was, fell at his feet, and said—with a hint of reproach in her voice—"Lord, if you had been here, my brother wouldn't have died."

When Jesus saw her crying, and the Judaeans who had come with her crying also, he was deeply disturbed. He asked, "Where have you laid him?"

They replied, "Master, come and see."

Overcome by both the sorrow that was present, and the pain he felt from their lack of understanding, Jesus wept. The Judaeans said, "See how much he loved him!" But some of them said, "He healed the eyes of the man born blind. Couldn't he have kept Lazarus from dying?"

Jesus was once more deeply moved, this time by anger, as he came to the tomb. It was a cave with a stone laid across the entrance. He spoke in a taut, firm voice, "Remove the stone."

Martha said, "Lord, the smell will be awful! He's been dead four days."

Jesus replied, "Didn't I tell you that if you believe, you will see G-d's glory?"

Martha nodded at the men of the village standing close by, and, reluctantly, they rolled away the stone. Jesus looked up and said, "Father, thank you for hearing me. I know you always hear me. I say this for the benefit of the crowd standing here, so that they will believe that you sent me."

Jesus then shouted with a loud voice, "Lazarus, come out!" The dead man shuffled out, his feet bound, his hands tied, and his face covered with a cloth. Jesus said to them, "Unbind him and let him go."

With shouts of joy and wonder, the sisters removed the grave clothes and received their brother into a bewildered embrace. Many of the Judaeans who came with Mary and saw what Jesus did believed in him. But some of them went to the Pharisees and reported what had happened. Then the chief priests and Pharisees called together the Sanhedrin and said, "What are we going to do? This man is doing many miraculous signs. If we let him go on like this, everyone will believe in him. Then the Romans will come and take away both our temple and our people."

Then the high priest of that year, named Caiaphas, told them, "You don't know anything! Don't you see that it is better for you that one man die for the people, than that the whole nation be destroyed?" He didn't say this out of his own insight: as high priest, he prophesied that Jesus would soon die for the nation—and not only for the nation. Jesus would also die so that G-d's children who were scattered everywhere would be gathered together as one.

From that day on, the high priests and Pharisees plotted and schemed to kill Jesus. Therefore, Jesus no longer moved about publicly among the Judaeans. Instead, he withdrew to a region near the desert, to a village called Ephraim, where he stayed with his disciples. When it was almost time for the Jewish Passover, many went up from the country to Yerushalayim for their ceremonial cleansing. They looked for Jesus, and, as they stood in the temple area, they asked one another, "What do you think? Isn't he coming to the feast at all?" But the chief priests and Pharisees had given orders that if anyone found out where Jesus was, he should report it to them, so that they might arrest him.

28

A Grand Entrance

JESUS KNEW THAT the time had finally come—the hour when the Son of Man would be glorified. He had set his face like flint toward Yerushalayim; everything he had done and taught had led to this moment. The authorities expected him to skulk into the city for Passover. But he had other plans. Plans set in place long before, through the words of the prophets.

As he approached Yerushalayim with his disciples, they came to Bethphage, the "house of early figs," and Bet Anya at the Mount of Olives. Jesus sent two of his disciples, saying to them, "Go to the village ahead of you, and just as you enter it, you will find a foal tied there, which no one has ever ridden. Untie it and bring it here. If anyone asks you, 'Why are you doing this?' tell him, 'The Master needs it and will send it back here shortly.'" When they entered the village they found the foal, just as Jesus had said.

They brought the foal to Jesus, threw their cloaks over it, and helped him climb onto its back. As Jesus mounted the animal, word began to spread that he was riding into town, and great excitement erupted everywhere. Some people started to spread their cloaks on the road, while others spread palm branches that they had cut in the fields. Many looked on with awe, others just with curiosity. What did it mean? Were the people re-enacting the victory celebration that had followed the Maccabees' successful retaking of Yerushalayim in battle, more than a century earlier? It almost looked like the parade for a new Roman governor—although the governor always entered the city on a war charger, not a lowly donkey.

Those who went ahead and those who followed behind sang the psalms of ascents, the pilgrimage psalms, praising G-d and crying out:

Hosanna!
Blessed is he who comes in the name of the Lord!
Blessed is the coming kingdom of our father David!
Hosanna in the highest!

With the songs of the crowds ringing in his ears, Jesus entered Yerushalayim and went straight to the temple. He looked around at everything, taking in all the activity going on there, including the trading and money-changing operations. What he saw infuriated him, but it was already late, and so he went out to Bet Anya with the Twelve.

The disciples were filled with both anticipation and fear. While they were proud of their association with Jesus, they were also apprehensive about what might happen next. Judas, especially, was excited, for when he saw Jesus ride into Yerushalayim on a donkey, he remembered the prophecy of Zechariah which had foretold of the coming King:

Say to the daughter of Zion,
"Behold, your King is coming to you,
gentle, and mounted on a donkey,
even on a colt, the foal of a beast of burden."

Surely, the time had come for Jesus to claim the throne of his people, and throw the Romans out of Judaea. Surely, the yoke of the oppressor was about to be broken, as Isaiah had foretold so long ago!

They arrived in Bet Anya six days before the Passover, and Lazarus gave another dinner in Jesus' honor. Martha served, while Lazarus was among those reclining at the table with Jesus. Then Mary brought out a pint of pure nard, the most expensive perfume. She poured it on Jesus' feet, wiping them with her hair, and the house was filled with the fragrance.

Judas Iscariot objected, "Why wasn't this perfume sold and the money given to the poor? It was worth a year's wages!" He did not say this primarily because he cared about the poor, but because he was the keeper of the money bag. From time to time, he would help himself to what was put into it, setting money aside for the revolt against Rome that he believed was imminent.

"Leave her alone," responded Jesus. "It was intended that she should save this perfume for the day of my burial. You will always have the poor among you, but you will not always have me." Meanwhile a large crowd of Judaeans found out that Jesus was there, and they came, not only because of him but also to see Lazarus, whom he had raised from the dead. So the chief priests made plans to kill Lazarus as well, for on account of him many more Judaeans were putting their faith in Jesus.

As they departed Bet Anya to return to Yerushalayim early the next morning, Jesus was hungry. Seeing a fig tree in the distance, he went to find out if it had any fruit. In the spring, one might have expected to find early fruit on the tree for which Bethphage was named. But when he reached it, he found only leaves, not the sweet figs that would come in the fall. Jesus said to the tree, "May no one ever eat fruit from you again," and his disciples heard him say it. He then walked down the Mount of Olives across the Kidron Valley, and over Mount Zion.

Once in Yerushalayim itself, Jesus entered the temple and caused quite a stir. He began driving out those who were buying and selling there. He overturned the tables of the money changers and the benches of those selling doves, and would not allow anyone to carry merchandise through the temple courts. And he spoke a prophetic word, saying, "Is it not written: 'My house will be called a house of prayer for all nations'? But you have made it 'a den of robbers.'"

Then some of the Judaeans demanded of him, "What miraculous sign can you show us to prove you have authority to do all this?"

Jesus' answer was enigmatic. "Destroy this temple, and I will raise it again in three days."

With a sneer one responded, "It has taken forty-six years to build this temple, and you are going to raise it in three days?"

The chief priests and the teachers of the law heard about this and redoubled their efforts to find a way to kill Jesus; they feared him because the crowds were amazed at his teaching. But Jesus had far too large a following for them to act in broad daylight, especially with throngs of pilgrims present for the Passover Festival. So they began to look for an opportune moment to do something in the dark of night.

The next morning, as Jesus and the disciples went along the same road into Yerushalayim from Bet Anya, the disciples noticed that the fig tree had withered from the roots. Cephas remembered and said to Jesus, "Master, look! The fig tree you cursed has withered!"

"Have faith in G-d," Jesus answered. "Amen, I say to you, if anyone says to this mountain, 'Go, throw yourself into the sea,' and does not doubt in his heart but believes that what he says will happen, it will be done for him. Therefore, I tell you, whatever you ask for in prayer, believe that you have received it, and it will be yours. And when you stand praying, if you hold anything against anyone, forgive him, so that your Father in heaven may forgive you your sins."

They arrived again in Yerushalayim at Mount Zion, and while Jesus was walking in the temple courts, the chief priests, the teachers of the Law, and the elders came to him. "By what authority are you doing these things?" they asked. "Who gave you authority to do this?"

Jesus replied, "I will ask you one question. Answer me, and I will tell you by what authority I am doing these things. John's baptism: Was it from heaven, or from humans? Tell me!"

They huddled and, in whispered discussion, concluded, "If we say, 'From heaven,' he will ask, 'Then why didn't you believe him?' But if we say, 'From humans . . .'" They feared the people, for everyone held that John was truly a prophet. So they turned back to Jesus and answered, "We don't know."

Jesus said, "Then neither will I tell you by what authority I am doing these things." He continued to teach boldly in the temple courts, drawing enormous crowds. On this day, especially because there were so many Galileans present with him, Jesus chose to tell the sort of parables they enjoyed so much.

"Tell me what you think," Jesus said to the authorities present. "There was a man who had two sons. He went to the first and said, 'Son, go and work today in the vineyard.' 'I will not,' the son answered, but later he changed his mind and went. Then the father went to the other son and said the same thing. He answered, 'I will, sir,' but he did not go. Which of the two did what his father wanted?"

"The first," they answered.

Jesus said to them, "Amen, I say to you, the tax collectors and the prostitutes are entering the kingdom of G-d ahead of you. For John came to you to show you the way of righteousness, and you did not believe him, but the tax collectors and the prostitutes did. And even after you saw this, you did not repent and believe him.

"Listen to another parable. A man planted a vineyard, put a fence around it, dug a pit for the winepress, and built a tower. Then he rented it to tenant farmers and took a trip. When it was time, he sent a servant to collect from the tenants his share of the fruit of the vineyard. But they grabbed the servant, beat him, and sent him away empty-handed. The landowner sent another servant to them, but they struck him on the head and treated him disgracefully. He sent another one; that one, they killed. The landlord sent many other servants, but the tenants beat some and killed others.

"Now the landowner had one son, whom he loved dearly. He sent him last of all, thinking, 'They will respect my son.' But those tenant farmers said to each other, 'This is the heir. Let's kill him, and the inheritance will be ours.' They grabbed him, killed him, and threw him out of the vineyard."

Every eye was on Jesus, and he was watching the priests and the scribes.

"So what will the owner of the vineyard do? He will come and destroy those tenants and give the vineyard to others."

When the elders of the people heard it, they cried out, "May it never be!"

Jesus looked at them and said, "Have you never read in the Scriptures, 'The stone the builders rejected has become the keystone; the Lord has done this, and it is marvelous in our eyes'? Therefore, I tell you that the kingdom of G-d will be taken away from you and given to a people who will produce its fruit. He who falls on this stone will be broken to pieces, but he on whom it falls will be crushed."

When the chief priests and the Pharisees heard Jesus' parables, they knew he was talking about them. They fumed, and looked for a way to arrest him, but they continued to be afraid of the crowd because the people held that Jesus was a prophet. So once again, they did nothing.

29

Teaching at the Table

IT WAS STILL several days before the Passover Feast. Jesus knew that the time had come for him to leave this world and go to the Father. Having loved his own who were in the world, he now was ready to show them the full extent of his love.

That evening, Jesus and the disciples once more enjoyed the hospitality of Lazarus' family in Bet Anya. After a lengthy conversation with his most beloved disciple, Jesus—knowing that the Father had given all things into his hands, and that he had come from G-d and was going back to G-d—got up from the meal, took off his outer clothing, and wrapped a towel around his waist. After that, he poured water into a basin and began to wash his disciples' feet, drying them with the towel that was wrapped around him. He came to Cephas, who said to him, "Master, are you going to wash *my* feet?"

Jesus replied, "You do not realize now what I am doing, but later you will understand."

"No," said Cephas, pulling his feet back from Jesus' hands, "you shall never wash my feet."

"Very well, Cephas, but unless I wash you, you have no part with me."

"Then, Master, not just my feet, but my hands and my head as well!"

"A person who has had a bath needs only to wash his feet; his whole body is clean. And you are clean . . . though not every one of you." Jesus knew who was going to betray him, and that was why he said not everyone was clean.

After he washed the disciples' feet, Jesus put on his robes and returned to his place at the table. He said to them, "Do you understand what I've done for you? You call me 'teacher' and 'Master,' and you speak correctly, because I am. If then, as your Master and teacher, I have washed your feet, you too must wash each other's feet. I have given you an example: just as I have done, you also must do. I assure you, servants aren't greater than their master, nor are those who are sent greater than the one who sent them. Since you know these things, you will be blessed if you do them."

Jesus paused, his eyes moving briefly to Judas Iscariot. With a heavy voice, he said, "But I'm not speaking about all of you. I know those whom I've chosen. But this is to fulfill the Scripture, 'The one who eats my bread has turned against me.' I'm telling you this now, before it happens, so that when it does happen you will believe that I Am. I assure you that whoever receives someone I send, receives me, and whoever receives me, receives the One who sent me."

After the table had been cleared, they poured more wine. Jesus began to teach them at some length. "Little children, I'm with you for a little while longer. You will look for me—but, just as I told the Judaeans, I also tell you now—'Where I'm going, you can't come.'

"I give you a new commandment. Love one another. Just as I have loved you, so you also must love each other. This is how everyone will know that you are my disciples, when you love each other."

Cephas said to Jesus, "Lord, where are you going?"

Jesus turned to him. "Where I am going, you can't follow me now, but you will follow later. Simon, Simon, listen! Satan has demanded to sift you all like wheat, but I have prayed for you, that your own faith may not fail."

Cephas began to object, but Jesus continued. "But once you've turned back—strengthen your brothers and sisters." The other disciples looked as concerned as Cephas over Jesus' words.

Jesus' face softened as he spoke again.

"Don't be troubled. Trust in G-d. Trust also in me. My Father's house has rooms to spare. If that weren't the case, would I have told you that I'm going to prepare a place for you? When I go to prepare a place for you, I will return and take you to be with me—so that where I am, you will be too. You know the way to the place I'm going."

Thomas interjected, "Lord, we don't know where you are going! How can we know the way?"

"I am the way, the truth, and the life. No one comes to the Father except through me. If you have really known me, you will also know the Father. From now on, you know him and you have seen him."

Philip said, "Lord, show us the Father; that will be enough for us."

"Don't you know me, Philip, even after I have been with you all this time? Whoever has seen me has seen the Father. How can you say, 'Show us the Father'? Don't you believe that I am in the

Father and the Father is in me? The words I have spoken to you, I don't speak on my own. The Father, who dwells in me, does his works. Trust me when I say that I am in the Father and the Father is in me, or at least believe on account of the works themselves. I assure you that whoever believes in me will do the works that I do. They will do even greater works than these because I am going to the Father. I will do whatever you ask for in my name, so that the Father can be glorified in the Son. When you ask me for anything in my name, I will do it.

"If you love me, you will keep my commandments. I will ask the Father, and he will send another Advocate who will be with you forever. This Advocate is the Spirit of Truth, whom the world can't receive because it neither sees him nor recognizes him. You know him, because he lives with you and will be with you."

Jesus saw that the disciples were still concerned, if not confused. His face softened once more, and he said, "I won't leave you as orphans. I will come to you. Soon the world will no longer see me, but you will see me. Because I live, you will live too. On that day, you will know that I am in my Father, you are in me, and I am in you. Whoever has my commandments and keeps them loves me. Whoever loves me will be loved by my Father, and I will love them and reveal myself to them."

Another Judas—not Judas Iscariot—asked, "Lord, why are you about to reveal yourself to us and not to the world? Why won't you assume the full public mantle of King?"

"Whoever loves me will keep my word. My Father will love them, and we will come to them and make our home with them. Whoever doesn't love me doesn't keep my words. The word that you hear isn't mine. It is the word of the Father who sent me. I have spoken these things to you while I am with you. The

Advocate, the Holy Spirit, whom the Father will send in my name, will teach you everything and will remind you of everything I told you.

"Peace I leave with you. My peace I give you. I do not give to you as the world gives. Don't be troubled or afraid. You have heard me tell you, 'I'm going away and returning to you.' If you loved me, you would be happy that I am going to the Father, because the Father is greater than me. I have told you before it happens, so that when it happens you will believe. I won't say much more to you because this world's ruler is coming. But he has nothing on me. Rather, he comes so that the world will know that I love the Father and do just as the Father has commanded me."

Jesus saw that a few of the disciples were becoming drowsy, as they were full of good food, wine, and his words. He smiled and said, "Come now; it is time for us to get some rest."

One among them did not lay his head down to rest that night. Judas Iscariot paced the courtyard restlessly, mulling over all that Jesus had said. He finally came to the conclusion that Jesus would not be leading the revolt against Rome that he had hoped for. Jesus' action in the temple had signaled coming judgment by G-d, but it had done nothing to initiate that judgment.

After such great hopes at the beginning of the week, Judas was now thoroughly disillusioned with Jesus. He was also still smarting from Jesus' critique of him when he took exception to Mary's extravagant gesture with the perfume. If Jesus was not going to be the Messiah, like David, who would cleanse the land and rule it with an iron hand, then he must be a great deceiver. A sudden thought struck him: *Or perhaps Jesus just needs someone to force his hand.* This idea began to take hold of Judas' troubled mind.

So it was that Judas Iscariot went to the chief priests and asked, "What are you willing to give me if I hand Jesus over to you?" They counted out for him thirty silver denarii. From then on, Judas watched for an opportunity to betray Jesus.

30

Sparring with the Authorities

IT WAS NOW mid-week, and Jesus continued to teach fearlessly in the temple courts, drawing huge crowds. But on this morning the Pharisees determined to trap him in his teaching. They sent their disciples to him along with the Herodians, those partisans of Herod Antipas from Galilee.

"Teacher," they said to Jesus, "we know that you're genuine and you don't worry about what people think. You don't show favoritism, but teach G-d's way as it really is. Does the Law allow people to pay taxes to Caesar or not? Should we pay taxes or not?"

Knowing exactly what they were doing, Jesus said, "Why are you testing me? Bring me a denarius. Show it to me." Someone held out a coin. Without touching it, Jesus said, "Whose image and inscription is this?"

Glancing down, they saw the face of the emperor looking blankly back at them. "Caesar's," they replied.

"Then give to Caesar what belongs to Caesar and to G-d what belongs to G-d." Jesus' response confused them, and they didn't know what to say in return.

Later that same morning, the Sadducees, who believed there would be no resurrection of the dead, came to Jesus and they, too, tried to trap him. "Teacher, Moses wrote for us that if a man's brother dies, leaving a widow but no children, the brother must marry the widow and raise up children for his brother. Now, there were seven brothers. The first one married a woman; when he died, he left no children. The second brother then married her and died without leaving any children. The third did the same. None of the seven left any children. Finally, the woman died. At the resurrection, when they all rise up, whose wife will she be? After all, all seven were married to her."

Jesus said to them, "Your logic is faulty, because you don't know either the Scriptures or G-d's power. When people rise from the dead, they won't marry nor will they be given in marriage. Instead, they will be like G-d's angels. As for the resurrection from the dead, haven't you read in the scroll of Moses, in the passage about the burning bush, how G-d said to Moses, 'I am the G-d of Abraham, the G-d of Isaac, and the G-d of Jacob'? He isn't the G-d of the dead, but of the living. You are *dead wrong*!"

When the crowds heard this, they were astonished at his teaching, and they enjoyed seeing the authorities bested at their own word games. Even some of the scribes recognized Jesus' wisdom and begrudgingly acknowledged it. "Teacher, you have spoken well."

Hearing that Jesus had silenced the Sadducees, the Pharisees decided to try once more to trap him. One of them, an expert in the Law, tested him with this question: "Which commandment is the most important of all?"

Jesus replied, "The most important one is, 'Listen, O Israel! Our G-d is the one Lord, and you must love the Lord your G-d with your whole heart, with all your being, with your whole mind, and with all your strength.' The second is this, 'You will love your neighbor as yourself.' No other commandment is greater than these."

The legal expert said to him, "Well said, teacher. You have truthfully said that G-d is one and there is no other beside him. And to love G-d with a whole heart, a full understanding, and all of one's strength, and to love one's neighbor as oneself, is much more important than all kinds of burnt offerings and sacrifices."

When Jesus saw that he had answered with wisdom, he said to him, "You aren't far from G-d's dominion." While the Pharisees were gathered together around him, Jesus said, "Now let me ask you a question. What do you think about the Messiah? Whose son is he?"

"The son of David," they replied.

"How is it then that David, speaking by the Spirit, calls him 'Lord'? For he says, 'The Lord said to my Lord: "Sit at my right hand until I put your enemies under your feet."' If then David calls him 'Lord,' how can he be his son?"

No one could say a word in reply, and for the rest of the morning, no one dared to ask him any more questions.

As he was leaving the temple, one of his disciples said to him, "Teacher, look! What awesome stones and buildings!"

Jesus responded, "Do you see these enormous buildings? Not one stone will be left upon another. All will be demolished. All this building by Herod and his successors will be wasted effort as it was not blessed by G-d, indeed not built by G-d, and so they labored in vain."

Jesus crossed over the Kidron Brook and climbed up to his favorite spot on the Mount of Olives, overlooking the temple precincts. As he sat there opposite the temple, Simon, James, John, and Andrew, disturbed by what he had just said, approached him privately. "Tell us, when will these things happen? And what will be the sign that all these things are about to come to an end?"

Jesus eyed them intently. "Watch out that no one deceives you. Many people will come in my name, saying, 'I'm the one!' They will deceive many people. When you hear of wars and reports of wars, don't be alarmed. These things must happen, but this isn't the end yet. Nations and kingdoms will fight against each other, and there will be earthquakes and famines in all sorts of places. These things are just the beginning of the suffering associated with the end.

"Watch out for yourselves. People will hand you over to the councils. You will be beaten in the synagogues. You will stand before governors and kings because of me, so that you can testify before them. First, the good news must be proclaimed to all the nations. When they haul you in and hand you over, don't worry ahead of time about what to answer or say. Instead, say whatever is given to you at that moment, for you aren't doing the speaking, but the Holy Spirit is."

Jesus shook his head sadly as he reminded them once more, "Brothers and sisters will hand each other over to death. A father will turn in his children. Children will rise up against their parents and have them executed. Everyone will hate you because of my name. But whoever stands firm until the end will be saved.

"When you see the abomination that causes desolation, which Daniel foretold, standing where it shouldn't be, then those in Judaea must escape to the mountains. Those on the roof shouldn't come down or enter their houses to grab anything. Those in the field shouldn't come back to grab their clothes. How terrible it will be at that time for women who are pregnant and for women who are nursing their children." He leaned forward. "Pray that it doesn't happen in winter! In those days, there will be great suffering such as the world has never before seen and will never again see. If the Lord hadn't shortened that time, no one would be rescued. But for the sake of the chosen ones, the ones whom G-d chose, he has cut short the time.

He took a drink from his water skin. "If someone says to you, 'Look, here's the Messiah,' or, 'There he is,' don't believe it. False messiahs and false prophets will appear, and they will offer signs and wonders in order to deceive, if possible, those whom G-d has chosen. But you—watch out! I've told you everything ahead of time.

"There will be a time, after the suffering of that distress, when, as the Scriptures say, 'the sun will become dark, and the moon won't give its light. The stars will fall from the sky, and the planets and other heavenly bodies will be shaken.' At that later time, people will see the Son of Man coming in the clouds with great power and glory. Then he will send the angels and gather together his chosen people from the four corners of the earth, from the end of the earth to the end of heaven.

"Now learn this parable from the fig tree. After its branch becomes tender and it sprouts new leaves, you know that summer is near. In the same way, when you see these things happening on the earth, you know that it's near, right at the door. Amen, I say to you, that this generation won't pass away until all these signs upon the earth happen, concluding with the fall of the temple. Heaven and earth will pass away, but my words will certainly not pass away.

"As for the things that will happen after those signs upon the earth—including the Son of Man's return—nobody knows when that day or hour will come, not the angels in heaven and not even the Son. Only the Father knows. Watch out! Stay alert! For you don't know when that time is coming. It's as if someone took a trip, left the household behind, and put the servants in charge, giving each one a job to do, and told the doorkeeper to stay alert. Therefore, watch! You don't know when the head of the household will come, whether in the evening or at midnight, or when the rooster crows in the early morning or at daybreak. Don't let him show up when you weren't expecting, and find you sleeping. What I say to you, I say to all: Watch!"

As the disciples tried to take all this in, they realized Jesus was speaking about events both on the near and more distant horizons. But what was this about the Son of Man coming back? Was this another enigmatic reference to the resurrection of the Son of Man? So much was unclear to them. The walk back to Bet Anya was a short one from where they stood, on top of the ridge of the Mount of Olives. It was nearing time for dinner, and doubtless, Jesus would use that occasion to say more. So the disciples refrained from questioning him.

31

Comforting Words

THE MEAL ON Wednesday evening was not elaborate, and the mood was more somber than celebratory. After two days of confrontation with the authorities and some people among the crowds, the disciples wondered what would come next. Particularly prominent in their minds was Jesus' parable about the workers in the vineyard and the son returning to the vineyard. Of course, ever since Isaiah wrote the original parable about the vineyard, Israel had been accustomed to viewing itself as G-d's vineyard. Once more, as Jesus sat up on the couch and began to instruct them, it was as if he could read their minds.

"I am the genuine vine, and my Father is the vineyard keeper. He removes any of my branches that don't produce fruit, and he trims any branch that produces fruit so that it will produce even more fruit. You are already trimmed because of the word I have spoken to you. Remain in me, and I will remain in you. A branch can't produce fruit by itself, but must remain in the vine. Likewise, you can't produce fruit unless you remain in me. I am the vine; you are the branches. If you remain in me, and I in you, then you will produce much fruit. Without me, you can't do anything. If you don't remain in me, you will be like a branch that is thrown out and dries up. Those branches are gathered up, thrown into a fire, and burned. If you remain in me and my words remain in you, ask for whatever you want and it will be done for you. My Father is glorified when you produce much fruit, and in this way prove that you are my disciples.

"As the Father loved me, I too have loved you. Remain in my love. If you keep my commandments, you will remain in my love, just as I kept my Father's commandments and remain in his love. I have said these things to you, so that my joy will be in you and your joy will be complete. This is my commandment: love each other just as I have loved you. No one has greater love than this: to give up one's life for one's friends." An intense emotion swept across Jesus' face, and he reached out to grasp Cephas' hand. The moment passed, and he continued teaching.

"And *you* are my friends, if you do what I command you. I don't call you servants any longer, because servants don't know what their master is doing. Instead, I call you friends, because everything I heard from my Father I have made known to you. You didn't choose me, but I chose you and appointed you so that you could go and produce fruit, and so that your fruit could last. As a result, whatever you ask the Father in my name, he will give you." His eyes held the gaze of each of the disciples in turn as he said, "This I command you: love one another.

"If the world hates you, know that it hated me first. If you belonged to the world, the world would love you as its own. However, I have chosen you out of the world, and you don't belong to the world. This is why the world hates you. Remember what I told you, 'Servants aren't greater than their master.' If the world harassed me, it will harass you too. If it kept my word, it will also keep yours. The world will do all these things to you on account of my name, because it doesn't know the One who sent me.

"If I hadn't come and spoken to the people of this world, they wouldn't be guilty of sin. But now they have no excuse for their sin. Whoever hates me also hates the Father. If I hadn't done works among them that no one else had done, they wouldn't be sinners. But now they have seen and hated both me and my Father. This fulfills the word written in their Law, 'They hated me without a reason.'

"When the Advocate comes, whom I will send from the Father—the Spirit of Truth who proceeds from the Father—he will testify about me. You also must testify, because you have been with me from the beginning.

"Now I am going to the Father who sent me, and none of you asks me where I am going. You are very sad from hearing all of this. But I tell you that I am going to do what is best for you. That is why I am going away. The Holy Spirit cannot come to help you until I leave. But after I am gone, I will send the Spirit to you. The Spirit will come and show the people of this world the truth about sin and G-d's justice and the judgment. The Spirit will show them that they are wrong about sin, because they didn't have faith in me. They are wrong about G-d's justice, because I am going to the Father, and you won't see me again. And they are wrong about the judgment, because G-d has already judged the ruler of this world."

Jesus looked at his disciples fondly. "I have much more to say, but right now it would be more than you could understand. The Spirit shows what is true, and will come and guide you into the full truth. I have used examples to explain to you what I have been talking about. But the time will come when I will speak to you plainly about the Father and will no longer use examples like these. You will ask the Father in my name, and I won't have to ask him for you. G-d the Father loves you because you love me, and you believe that I have come from him. I came from the Father into the world and am returning to the Father."

The disciples said, "Now you are speaking plainly to us! You are not using examples. At last we know that you understand everything, and we don't need to question you. Now we believe that you truly have come from G-d."

Jesus replied, "Do you really believe me? The time will come—and is already here—when all of you will be scattered. Each of you will go back home and leave me by myself. But the Father will be with me, and I won't be alone. I have told you this, so that you may have peace in your hearts because of me. While you are in the world, you will suffer. But take courage! I have overcome the world."

As the lamps burned low, and heads lowered onto chests, Jesus concluded the evening with a prayer. He looked toward heaven, lifted up his hands, and prayed.

"Father, the time has come. Glorify your Son, so that the Son can glorify you. You gave him authority over everyone so that he could give eternal life to everyone you gave him. This is eternal life: to know you, the only true G-d, and Jesus Christ whom you sent. I have glorified you on earth by finishing the work you gave me to do. Now, Father, glorify me in your presence with the glory I shared with you before the world was created.

"I have revealed your name to the people you gave me from this world. They were yours and you gave them to me, and they have kept your word. Now they know that everything you have given me comes from you. This is because I gave them the words that you gave me, and they received them. They truly understood that I came from you, and they believed that you sent me.

"I'm praying for them. I'm not praying for the world but for those you gave me, because they are yours. Everything that is mine is yours and everything that is yours is mine; I have been glorified in them. I'm no longer in the world, but they are in the world, even as I'm coming to you. Holy Father, watch over them in your name, the name you gave me, that they will be one just as we are one. When I was with them, I watched over them in your name, the name you gave to me, and I kept them safe. None of them were lost, except the one who was destined for destruction, so that Scripture would be fulfilled.

"Now I'm coming to you, and I say these things while I'm in the world so that they can share completely in my joy. I gave your word to them and the world hated them, because they don't belong to this world, just as I don't belong to this world. I'm not asking that you take them out of this world, but that you keep them safe from the Evil One. They don't belong to this world, just as I don't belong to this world. Make them holy in the truth; your word is truth. As you sent me into the world, so I have sent them into the world. I made myself holy on their behalf, so that they also would be made holy in the truth.

"I'm not praying only for them but also for those who believe in me because of their word. I pray they will be one, Father, just as you are in me and I am in you. I pray that they also will be in us, so that the world will believe that you sent me. I've given them the glory that you gave me, so that they can be one just as we are one. I'm in them and you are in me, so that they will be made perfectly one. Then the world will know that you sent me and that you have loved them just as you loved me.

"Father, I want those you gave me to be with me where I am. Then they can see my glory, which you gave me because you loved me before the creation of the world. Righteous Father, even the world didn't know you, but I've known you, and these believers know that you sent me. I've made your name known to them and will continue to make it known, so that your love for me will be in them, and I myself will be in them."

The prayer was long, but heartfelt, and the disciples felt comforted by it, and yet they also had a heightened sense of foreboding. It seemed clear that Jesus was telling them that his ministry was coming to an end. But where was he going? And why couldn't they come with him?

As they rose to head to where they would lie down for the night, Jesus told them that they would celebrate the Passover the following night, and that Lazarus had arranged a place for them to do so within the city walls. In order not to draw too much attention, an arrangement had been made that there would be a special signal and a person for them to follow, so they would know where to go. This puzzled the disciples even more, since Friday evening, in this case, should be both Shabbat and the beginning of Passover; so why would they celebrate the meal on *Thursday* evening, the beginning of the Day of Preparation, the day of the slaughtering of the lambs? None of it was clear. But Jesus said nothing further, and the disciples were afraid to ask.

32

Widows

THE FOLLOWING MORNING, Jesus sat on some steps in the temple courts and began to teach his disciples as the people listened in. From his vantage point, he could see the place where people came to throw money into the vessels called temple treasuries. These were large fluted vessels made of stone into which it was easy to drop coins. As some Pharisees passed by, Jesus pointed them out to the disciples.

"Watch out for the teachers of the Law. They like to walk around in long robes and want to be greeted with honor in the marketplace. They long for places of honor in the synagogues and at banquets. Yet these are the ones who cheat widows out of their homes, and make a show of offering long prayers. They will be judged most harshly."

Jesus fell silent for a while and observed the crowd putting their money into the temple treasuries. Often, a rich person would throw in a large amount, which no doubt made a very satisfying jingle as it hit the pile below. But as Jesus watched, a poor widow came and put in two very small copper coins, worth only a fraction of a penny. They landed silently. Pointing out the woman to his disciples, Jesus said, with more than a hint of anger in his voice, "Amen, I say to you, this poor widow has put more into the treasury than all the others. They all gave out of their wealth; but she, out of her poverty, put in everything that she had left to live on.

"Let me tell you another parable. In a certain city there was a judge who neither feared G-d nor respected people. In that city there was a widow who kept coming to him, asking, 'Give me justice in this case against my adversary.' For a while the judge refused, but he finally said to himself, 'I don't fear G-d or respect people, but I will give this widow justice because she keeps bothering me. Otherwise, there will be no end to her coming here and embarrassing me.'"

Jesus looked around the crowd. "Listen to what the unjust judge says. Won't G-d provide justice to his chosen people who cry out to him day and night? Will he be slow to help them? I tell you, he will give them justice quickly. Ah, but when the Son of Man comes, will he find faithfulness on the earth?"

Some of Jesus' female disciples—Miryam, Joanna, Susanna, and a few others—had come down to Yerushalayim with the Twelve for the festival, and they expressed great appreciation for this teaching. Was it not deeply in agreement with the many exhortations in Torah about taking care of widows? The women had also been staying in Bet Anya, with a family well known to Mary and Martha, and had been present at most of the teaching sessions in Lazarus' home and on the Temple Mount.

They noted that Jesus seemed very sad on this day. As he looked out over the temple courts, he lamented, "O Yerushalayim, Yerushalayim, you who kill the prophets and stone those who were sent to you! How often I have wanted to gather your people, just as a hen gathers her chicks under her wings. But you didn't want that. Look, your house is abandoned. I tell you, you won't see me until the time comes when you say, 'Blessings on the one who comes in the Lord's name.'

"If you, even you, had only known on this day what would bring you peace. But now it is hidden from your eyes. The days will come upon you when your enemies will build a siege wall against you and encircle you and hem you in on every side. They will dash you to the ground, you and the children within your walls. They will not leave one stone on another, because you did not recognize the time of G-d's coming to you."

Jesus did not stay long in the temple courts on this day, but went across to the Garden of Gethsemane to pray during the afternoon. The plan was that late in the afternoon, all the disciples would gather at the house of Lazarus and then follow directions to the place where they would celebrate the Passover with Jesus.

33

A Final Meal

THE AFTERNOON PASSED quickly, and the rendezvous at Bet Anya happened without incident. Jesus' hour was swiftly approaching, and so he sent two of his disciples ahead, telling them, "Go into the city, and a man carrying a jar of water will meet you. Follow him. Say to the owner of the house where he enters, 'The teacher asks, "Where is my guest room, where I may eat the Passover with my disciples?"' He will show you a large upper room, furnished and ready. Make preparations for us there." The disciples left, went into the city, and found things just as Jesus had told them. So they prepared for this very strange Passover meal.

When evening came, Jesus arrived with the Twelve. While they were reclining at the table eating, he said, "Amen, I say to you, one of you will betray me, one who is eating with me." They were deeply saddened, and looked at each other in disbelief. One by one, they said to him, "Surely it's not me, is it?"

Jesus answered them, "It is one of the Twelve, one who is dipping bread with me into this bowl. The Son of Man goes to his death just as it is written about him. But how terrible it is for that person who betrays the Son of Man! It would have been better for him if he had never been born."

Judas Iscariot, who was reclining directly to Jesus' left, regarded the bread he had in his hand, and then looked directly at Jesus. Jesus said softly, "Hurry and do what you're determined to do." Judas looked surprised, held Jesus' gaze for a long moment, and then slipped out quickly into the night. The other disciples were surprised by this behavior, but thought that perhaps Jesus had sent him on an errand.

A profound heaviness hung over the celebration of this oddly early Passover meal, almost as if the death angel of old was passing by just outside the door. Only on this night, there was no protective blood on the lintel above the door. Jesus himself seemed burdened with the weight of the world, encumbered with enormous cares. He didn't seem much in the mood to celebrate or even to eat. While the disciples ate quietly, Jesus bowed his head—in prayer? in pain?—and then reached for a basket of flatbread.

Jesus took a loaf, blessed it, broke it, and gave it to them, saying, "Take, eat; this is my body." They passed the loaf among them, once again confused by Jesus' words. Then Jesus took a cup, gave thanks, and gave it to them, and they all drank from it. He said to them, "This is my blood of the new covenant, which is poured out for many for forgiveness of sins. Amen, I say to you, that I won't drink the fruit of the vine again until that day when I drink it in a new way with you in G-d's dominion."

No one really understood why Jesus had reinterpreted the elements of the ritual meal, and it was too formal an occasion to allow for questions or dialogue. So it was that when they had sung a solemn hymn about the Passover lamb and the angel, they went out to the Mount of Olives.

Jesus sat down on the grass at one of his favorite spots on the mount. Looking at his disciples, moving his gaze slowly from one to the next, he said, "You will all fall away, for it is written, 'I will strike the shepherd, and the sheep will be scattered.' But after I have risen, I will go ahead of you into Galilee."

Cephas declared boldly, "Even if all fall away, *I* will not."

Jesus regarded Cephas with affection—and sadness. "Amen, I say to you, that this very night, before the rooster crows twice, you yourself will disown me three times."

But Cephas insisted emphatically, "Even if I have to die with you, I will never disown you." And all the others said the same.

Moving down toward the bottom of the Mount of Olives, they went to a place called Gethsemane, or "oil press," for there was a small press set up in the grove of olive trees at this spot. Jesus said to his disciples, "Sit here while I pray." He took Cephas, James, and John along with him, and they could see that he was deeply distressed and troubled.

"My soul is overwhelmed with sorrow to the point of death," he said to the three. "Stay here and keep watch with me."

Going a little farther, he fell to the ground and prayed that, if it were possible, this hour might pass him by—that the cup of G-d's judgment on sin might pass from him. "My Abba, my Father, everything is possible for you. Take this cup of suffering away from me. Yet not what I want, but what you want."

The enormity and horror of what was about to happen to him were crystal clear to Jesus. When he told the disciples he was going to be killed, he had not mentioned crucifixion. Crucifixion was the most cruel and shameful way possible to die under the rule of Rome. It was a deliberate, public humiliation, a public shaming, a person being stripped naked before being hoisted up on display.

There could be no more ignoble or less redemptive way to die for a Jew. Indeed, many Jews saw it as a sign of G-d's final judgment on a life, a sign that one was cursed. They even read a scripture from Deuteronomy as speaking directly to this terrible fate: "Cursed is he who hangs upon a tree." There was also a widespread belief that how one died most revealed one's character.

Such thoughts flashed through Jesus' mind as he went apart to pray to G-d, praying as he had never prayed before. So intensely had he set to the task of praying and so distressed was he, that he began sweating even in the cool of a Judaean hill country evening, sweating profusely, the sweat beading upon his brow like great drops of blood. The thought of crucifixion horrified Jesus. Not only because it meant certain death—for he fully understood that he would die. Not only because of the public humiliation and shame—though that was on his mind. But most profoundly because he fully realized that if his death was to be a ransom for many, if his death was to be an atonement for sins, then the full weight of G-d's judgment on sin would fall on him. He would be both scapegoat and Passover lamb, taking away the sins of the world. It meant that he would die utterly alone, forsaken by friends and family. But would he also be forsaken by his Abba? To die the death of an infamous sinner was shame enough, but to die abandoned by one and all was almost too horrific to contemplate. Yet he had to wrestle with these thoughts, because they tormented his increasingly tortured mind.

After what seemed like hours, Jesus returned to his disciples and found them sleeping. "Cephas, are even you asleep? Could you not keep watch for one hour? Watch and pray so that you will not fall into temptation. The spirit is willing, but the body is weak."

Once more, he went away and prayed the same prayer. When he came back, he again found them sleeping, because their eyes were heavy. They did not know what to say to him. He went away to pray a third time, and upon returning, he looked up to see a procession of torches making their way up the hill, and called out to his disciples, "Are you still sleeping and resting? Enough! The hour has come. Look, the Son of Man is betrayed into the hands of sinners. Rise! Let us go! Here comes my betrayer!"

The disciples rose, rubbing the sleep from their eyes, and saw Judas approach Jesus. Behind him they could see a crowd armed with swords and clubs, sent from the chief priests, the teachers of the Law, and the elders. The betrayer had arranged a signal with them: 'The one I kiss is the man; arrest him and lead him away under guard.' Going at once to Jesus, Judas said, "Master!" and kissed him on the cheek, before turning swiftly aside. The men seized Jesus to arrest him.

Then Cephas, who had a sword, drew it and swung wildly at the high priest's servant, a man named Malchus, cutting off his right ear. Jesus commanded Cephas, "Put your sword away! Shall I not drink the cup the Father has given me? No more of this!" And he touched the man's ear and healed him.

Jesus turned to the elders of his people, their faces cloaked in darkness behind the guards. "Am I leading a rebellion that you have come out with swords and clubs to capture me? Every day this week I was with you, teaching in the temple courts, and you did not arrest me. But the Scriptures must be fulfilled."

The disciples looked at Jesus, and then as one they fled. Two of the disciples—Cephas and Lazarus—ran only a little distance away, hiding behind one of the ancient olive trees and watching to see what would happen next.

The captors took Jesus to the high priest, and all the chief priests, elders, and teachers of the Law came together. Cephas and the beloved disciple carefully followed, some distance behind, for Lazarus already knew where they would take Jesus. He went into the high priest's courtyard, right behind the guards, but Cephas had to wait outside at the door. Lazarus, who was known to the high priest, then returned and spoke to the girl on duty, who brought Cephas in. There he sat with the guards, who were warming themselves by the fire.

The chief priests and members of the Sanhedrin looked for evidence against Jesus so that they could put him to death, but they could not find any. Many testified falsely against him, but their statements did not agree—and the Law was clear that the testimony of at least two of them had to conform to each other before their word could be accepted as trustworthy and true. Then some others stood up, those who had been part of the crowd listening to Jesus earlier in the week, and gave this false testimony against him: "We heard him say, 'I will destroy this man-made temple and in three days will build another, not made by man.'" Yet even their testimony did not agree.

Then the high priest, Caiaphas, stood up before them and asked Jesus, "Are you not going to answer? What is this testimony that these men are bringing against you?" But Jesus remained silent.

So it was that Caiaphas, to force the issue, asked him, "*Are you the Messiah, the Son of the Blessed One?*"

"I am," said Jesus, simply. Then he spoke in a clear voice that rang throughout the marbled hall. "And you will see the Son of Man sitting at the right hand of the Mighty One and coming on the clouds of heaven!"

The high priest tore his clothes. "Why do we need any more witnesses? You have heard the blasphemy. What do you think?" It was not the claim to be the Messiah that prompted Caiaphas' dramatic response, for many had made such a claim. Instead, it was Jesus' claim to be the coming Son of Man—who had G-d's role of judging the earth and who would rule forever on it. Having failed to secure condemnation from the testimony of the "witnesses" he brought before the council, Caiaphas seized on Jesus' own words, for surely they supplied the condemnation he needed.

The majority of the assembly agreed with the high priest, and so they condemned Jesus as worthy of death. And then the humiliation began. Some began to spit at him. They blindfolded him, struck him with their fists, and said mockingly, "Prophesy!" The guards added blows of their own.

While Jesus endured the first of what would be many beatings that night, Cephas—unaware of what was happening inside the palace—sat below in the courtyard, still warming himself by a brazier. One of the servant girls of the high priest came by. When she saw Cephas she paused and examined his face. Then she said, "You, also, were with that Netzerene, Jesus."

Cephas denied her claim. "I don't know or understand what you're talking about," he said, and went out into the entryway. But the servant girl followed him, and she said to those standing around, "This fellow is one of them." Again, Cephas denied it.

After a little while, those standing near said to Cephas, "Surely you *are* one of them, for you are a Galilean—your accent gives you away." He began to call down curses on himself, and he swore to them, "I don't know this man you're talking about."

Immediately, a rooster in the distance crowed for a second time. Then Cephas remembered the words Jesus had spoken to him: "Before the rooster crows twice, you will disown me three times." And he broke down and wept.

34

The Truth on Trial

JESUS WAS COMPLETELY alone now, having been abandoned by all his Galilean male disciples. Lazarus, though he had not abandoned Jesus, and had indeed gained access to Caiaphas' house, had not been able to stem the tide against Jesus. Near dawn, when the meeting was over, the leaders of the whole assembly rose and led Jesus off to the Roman procurator, Pontius Pilate. Knowing that Pilate would not respond to accusations of someone merely breaking Jewish law or claiming to be some prophesied religious figure, they went to Pilate prepared to claim that Jesus was seditious.

By now it was early morning, and to avoid becoming ceremonially unclean—because they wanted to eat the Passover meal later that day—the Jewish authorities did not enter the governor's palace. So Pilate had to come out to them, something which did not incline him to grant whatever request they planned to make. When he saw the gathered dignitaries and their bloodied victim, he demanded, "What charges are you bringing against this man?"

"If he were not a criminal," they replied, "we would not have handed him over to you."

Pilate, exasperated because his docket was already full of cases, said dismissively, "Take him yourselves, and judge him by your own law."

"But we have no right to execute anyone," they objected. Seeing that Pilate was about to summarily dismiss them, they called out, "We found this man misleading our people, telling them not to pay taxes to Caesar, and saying that he himself is the Anointed One, a king."

Pilate looked at the religious leaders, then snapped his fingers, and two soldiers laid hands on Jesus and brought him inside the praetorium. Pilate regarded the man standing before him for quite some time. Was this fellow another Barabbas—a bandit leader recently caught, and languishing in chains in the cells? No, he had a different look about him. Pilate sensed no hostility coming from Jesus. Finally, he asked, "Well? Are you the king of the Jews?"

Jesus answered, "Do you say this on your own or have others spoken to you about me?" Insulted, Pilate responded, "I'm not a Jew, am I? Your nation and its chief priests handed you over to me. What have you done?"

"My kingdom doesn't originate from this world. If it did, my disciples would fight so that I wouldn't have been arrested by the Jewish authorities. My kingdom isn't from here."

"Aha! So you *are* a king?"

"You are right in saying that I am a king. I was born and came into the world for this reason: to testify to the truth. Whoever accepts the truth listens to my voice."

"And what exactly is truth?" Pilate asked sarcastically. Getting no response, he asked, "Where are you really from?" Jesus didn't answer. Pilate slammed his hand down on the arm of his chair.

"You won't speak to me? Don't you know that I have authority to either release you or crucify you?"

Jesus regarded the Roman calmly. "You would have no authority over me if it had not been given to you from above. That's why the one who handed me over to you has the greater sin."

Pilate held Jesus' gaze for a while before making the decision to release him. He saw no threat in the man. So he went out to the Jewish authorities and said, "I find no basis for a charge against him. But it is your custom for me to release to you one prisoner at the time of the Passover. Do you want me to release this so-called 'king of the Jews'?"

"No!" They cried. One of the chief priests stepped forward. "He stirs up the people all over Judaea by his teaching. He started in Galilee and has come all the way here."

"So the man is a Galilean?" asked Pilate. Seeing a way to get this man off his hands, he declared, "Then he falls under Herod's jurisdiction. I understand that Herod is in the city for your festival. Send him there. Let Herod deal with this matter."

Now, when Herod saw Jesus, he was greatly pleased, because he had wanted to see Jesus for a long time. From what he had heard about him, he hoped to see him perform a miracle. He plied him with many questions, but Jesus gave him no answer. The chief priests and the teachers of the Law were standing there, vehemently accusing him. But they, too, garnered no response. Then Herod and his soldiers ridiculed and mocked him. Dressing him in an elegant robe, they sent him back to Pilate. That day Herod and Pilate became allies; before this they had been antagonistic toward each other.

Pilate called together the chief priests, the rulers, and the people, and said to them, "You brought me this man as one who was inciting the people to rebellion. I have examined him in your presence and have found no basis for your charges against him. Neither has Herod, for he sent him back to us; as you can see, he has done nothing to deserve death. Therefore, I will flog him and then release him."

With one voice they cried out, "Away with this man! Release Barabbas to us!" Pilate shook his head in amazement. Release Barabbas? A murderer? No, he had no desire to release Barabbas. Wanting to release Jesus, Pilate appealed to them again. But they kept shouting, "Crucify him! Crucify him!"

For the third time he spoke to them. "Why? What crime has this man committed? I have found in him no grounds for the death penalty. Therefore, I will have him punished and then release him." But at this point, one among the Jewish authorities cried out, "If you don't execute this man, then you are no friend of Caesar's, for this man claims to be a king."

Now this struck a nerve with Pilate. He knew that if another Jewish delegation was sent to Tiberius complaining of the way he conducted affairs in Yerushalayim, he might well lose what he had worked so hard to gain—the favor of the emperor and the possibility of better appointments after serving in this miserable province. So Pilate reluctantly decided to grant their demand. He released the man who had been thrown into prison for insurrection and murder, this Barabbas—or "son of the father"—and instead surrendered Jesus to their will. He was far more concerned about preserving his status than in seeing justice was done in this matter.

Thus it was that, because Pilate heard the words, "Anyone who claims to be a king opposes Caesar," he brought Jesus out and sat down on the judge's seat at a place known as the Stone Pavement, which in Aramaic is "*Gabbatha.*"

Pilate addressed the small crowd gathered outside the praetorium—for it was still early in the morning of the Day of Preparation—and said, "Here is your king," clearly mocking the Jewish authorities who looked on.

The crowd took up the shout, "Crucify him! Crucify him!"

"Shall I crucify your king?" Pilate retorted.

But the response to his question did not come from the crowd. It came from the chief priests: "We have no king but Caesar!"

Pilate's jaw dropped in disbelief. Even the crowd became quiet at this—surely blasphemous—declaration. When Pilate saw the depth of this charade, he suddenly had no further wish to be part of it. But *he* would have the last word, not these arrogant priests.

He called a centurion over, and spoke loudly enough for all gathered to hear his words: "When you take this man to be crucified, I want you to fasten this *titulus* (the notice of the crime that the person being executed had committed) to the top of the cross: 'JESUS OF NETZERIT, THE KING OF THE JEWS.' And inscribe those words in Hebrew, Latin, and Greek."

When the chief priests heard this, they strenuously objected. "Do not write, 'The King of the Jews,' but that this man *claimed* to be king of the Jews."

Pilate replied, "What I have written, I have written." Then he called for a bowl of water and washed his hands of the whole sorry affair. He ordered Barabbas released, and after having Jesus scourged, handed him over to the centurion to be taken to Golgotha, the place of execution outside the city walls.

When Judas, who had betrayed him, saw that Jesus was condemned, he was seized with remorse and returned the thirty silver denarii to the chief priests and the elders. "I have sinned," he told them, "for I have betrayed innocent blood."

"What is that to us?" they said with a sneer. "That's your responsibility."

So Judas threw the money into the temple and left. Then he went away and hanged himself. When the coins were brought to the chief priests, they said, "It is against the Law to put this into the treasury, since it is blood money." So they decided to use the money to buy the potter's field as a burial place for foreigners. That is why it has been called the *Hakeldama*, "the Field of Blood," to this day.

35

The Death of the Son of Man

AS THE ROMAN soldiers led Jesus away, they seized a man named Simon, from Cyrene, a Roman colony on the north coast of Africa. Simon was a faithful Jew of the Diaspora—those who lived beyond the borders of ancient Israel and were spread throughout the empire. He had come to Yerushalayim to celebrate the festival, and was on his way to purchase a lamb for Passover when the soldiers requisitioned his strong back, putting the crossbeam on his shoulders and making him carry it behind Jesus, who was barely able to stumble along.

A large crowd followed them, including women who were friends of Mary and Martha and had been present when Jesus raised Lazarus from the dead. Jesus turned to the women, who were mourning and wailing, and said to them through his wounded lips, "Daughters of Yerushalayim, do not weep for me; weep for yourselves and for your children. For the time will come when you will say, 'Blessed are the barren women, the wombs that never bore and the breasts that never nursed!' Then they will say to the mountains, 'Fall on us!' and to the hills, 'Cover us!' For if men do these things when the tree is green, what will happen when it is dry?"

When they came to the place called Golgotha, the Place of the Skull—so called because of the shape of the rock outcropping on this hill—they crucified Jesus, along with two revolutionaries: one on his right, the other on his left.

One soldier offered Jesus wine mixed with myrrh in order to lessen the pain, but Jesus did not take it. Dividing up his clothes, the soldiers cast lots to see what each would get. It was about the third hour, or nine in the morning, when they crucified him.

As the hours passed, people drew closer and closer to the crucified Jesus, growing ever bolder. Many of those who passed by hurled insults at him, shaking their heads in mockery and saying, "So, you who are going to destroy the temple and rebuild it in three days, come down from the cross and save yourself!"

In the same way, some of the chief priests and the teachers of the Law mocked him among themselves. "He saved others," they said, "but he can't save himself! Let this so-called Messiah, this king of Israel, come down now from the cross, that we may see and believe."

One of those crucified with him also heaped insults upon him, but the other revolutionary objected. "Don't you fear G-d, since you are under the same sentence of death? We are being punished justly, for we are getting what our deeds deserve. But this man has done nothing wrong." Then he turned his face to Jesus. "Jesus, remember me when you come into your dominion." Jesus answered him, "Amen, I say to you, today you will be with me in paradise." He was speaking of the highest level in heaven.

The man dropped his head, a slight smile parting his lips. The other spat in disgust.

At the sixth hour—noon—darkness came over the whole land, the sun obscured, and it remained so until the ninth hour. At about the ninth hour, Jesus cried out in a loud voice, "*Eloi, Eloi, lama sabachthani*?" which means, "My G-d, my G-d, why have you forsaken me?"

When some of those standing near heard this, they said, "Listen, he's calling Elijah." A bystander snorted out loud. "Well, let's see if Elijah comes to take him down."

If Jesus heard this exchange, he gave no indication of it. Instead, he looked down at the soldiers standing guard at the foot of the cross. He said, "Father, forgive them, for they do not know what they are doing."

It was at this juncture that some of Jesus' family and disciples arrived, having heard the rumor late that morning that Jesus was being executed. None of the male disciples from Galilee were present, but the female disciples—Miryam of Migdal, Joanna, Susanna, and others—were there, standing near enough to hear what was happening. Lazarus, the beloved disciple, had summoned up his courage and was also present, and the female disciples had gone to the home of Mary and Martha to tell Jesus' mother what was happening. Jesus' brothers and sisters were staying with cousins in the city.

At the ninth hour, under a pitch-black sky, the women stood as close to the cross of Jesus as the soldiers would allow. Jesus' mother had arrived, and when Jesus saw her with the disciple whom he loved standing nearby, he said to her, "Woman, here is your son," and to the disciple, "Here is your mother." Thus Jesus honored and provided for his mother with nearly his last breath. From that time on, Lazarus took her into his home.

Jesus knew that he had now finished his work. In order to fulfill the Scriptures, he said, "I am thirsty." A jar of cheap wine was there. Someone soaked a sponge with the wine and held it up to Jesus' mouth on the stem of a hyssop plant. After Jesus drank the wine, he said, "It is finished."

Suddenly a violent wind whipped up dust all around them, and in the city at that moment, the great curtain of the temple was torn in two from top to bottom. There was an enormous thunderclap, and Jesus called out with a loud voice, "Father, into your hands I commit my spirit." When he had said this, he breathed his last. Torrents of rain began to pelt down from the sky above.

The centurion overseeing the crucifixions had marveled at the way Jesus had not railed against G-d or his tormentors, unlike most people he nailed to crosses. As Jesus slowly released his last breath, the Roman exclaimed, "Surely, this man was a son of G-d."

When all the people who had gathered to witness Jesus' death saw what took place, they beat their breasts and went away. But those who knew him—including the rest of the women who had followed him from Galilee—stood at a distance, watching these things under the soaking rain. Because the Jewish authorities did not want the bodies left on the crosses during Shabbat, much less during Passover, they sent word to Pilate to have the soldiers break the legs of the three men to hasten their deaths, and then bring the bodies down.

The soldiers, therefore, came and broke the legs of the first man who had been crucified with Jesus, and then those of the other. But when they came to Jesus and found that he was already dead, they did not break his legs. Instead, one of the soldiers pierced Jesus' side with a spear, bringing a sudden flow of blood and water. Lazarus had stayed with Jesus' mother to the end—as she refused to move until then—and so he, too, witnessed all of this.

36

A Hasty Burial

NOT EVERY MEMBER of the Sanhedrin was pleased to hear the report of Jesus' death. Two men had abstained from the process of hastily condemning him: Joseph of Arimathea, and Nicodemus, who had talked to Jesus at Lazarus' house. Joseph was a good and upright man, waiting for the dominion of G-d, and he had not consented to the council's decision and action. After the crucifixion, he went to the praetorium and boldly asked Pilate for the body of Jesus.

With Pilate's permission—much to Joseph's surprise and relief—he went to Golgotha and took Jesus' body away. Nicodemus accompanied him, bringing a mixture of about seventy-five pounds of myrrh and aloes, for there had not been time to make the usual careful preparations. The two of them wrapped the body with the spices in strips of linen, to retard the odor, so that those who wanted to do so could come and grieve at the tomb during the week of mourning. This was in accordance with Jewish burial customs.

Near the place where Jesus was crucified, there was a garden, and in the garden there was a new tomb, in which no one had ever been laid and which belonged to Joseph. Because it was the end of the Day of Preparation and since the tomb was nearby, he and Nicodemus laid Jesus there. The women who had come with Jesus from Galilee followed them and saw the tomb and how his body was laid in it. Then they went back to where they were staying and prepared spices and perfumes so that they might also honor Jesus in burial. But they rested on Shabbat in obedience to the commandment.

The brothers of Jesus had attended the Passover Festival but had not been with their mother, who was staying with some of Jesus' friends from Bet Anya whom James and Joses did not know. It was only after the fact that Jesus' brothers and sisters learned of his execution, and while the news was not a total surprise, it was still traumatizing. On Shabbat, James sought out his mother to see what plans would need to be made for the family going forward, but when he found her, she was in no condition to think about the future. She had been with Jesus to the bitter end and, according to her and Lazarus, Jesus had requested at the last that Lazarus take her into his own home. This both shocked and upset James, and all he had been able to say was, "You mean you're not coming back to Galilee with us?"

Dressed in borrowed mourning clothes, Mary simply shook her head and said she would honor the testament Jesus had made from the cross, at least for now. She would stay with Lazarus. James was beside himself with anger at Jesus, despite knowing all that Jesus had endured. Partly this was because of the strange arrangement Jesus had made for the ongoing well-being of their mother, but also because Jesus was dead and wouldn't have to suffer the shame and suspicion of having a family member executed on a Roman cross. The rest of them would have to live with it, and foremost of those would be James, who was now head of the family.

All of these things cast a pall over the Shabbat and festival activities that the family would normally have taken part in. Mary wasn't eating, and no one felt like singing or celebrating. Lazarus tried to comfort James, but James shrugged him off, and abruptly left the house in Bet Anya. Saturday was a much quieter, less eventful day in Yerushalayim. No executions, no business in the temple, no merchants in the streets hawking their wares, no Roman soldiers marching around. All was quiet. Deathly quiet.

37

Resurrection

EARLY ON THE first day of the week, while it was still dark, Miryam of Migdal and the other Galilean women went to the tomb only to find that the stone had been removed from the entrance. Miryam then ran all the way down the Hinnom Valley to the path that led to Bet Anya, where she alerted Cephas and Lazarus, who were now leading the Galilean and Judaean disciples, respectively. When she saw them she blurted out, "They've taken the Master out of the tomb, and we don't know where they've put him!"

So Cephas and Lazarus started for the tomb. Both men hurried, but Lazarus reached the tomb first, not least because he knew exactly where Joseph had buried him. He bent over, looked inside, and saw the strips of linen lying discarded, but did not go in.

Cephas arrived, out of breath, and without hesitating went straight into the tomb. He, too, saw the strips of linen, as well as the burial cloth that had been around Jesus' head. The cloth was folded up, separate from the linen. Then Lazarus followed him inside. He saw and believed that G-d had done something remarkable; perhaps G-d had even taken Jesus directly up into heaven, which Jesus had seemed to indicate several nights earlier. But still, even Lazarus—with his own experience behind him—did not understand what the Scriptures had said, that Jesus must rise from the dead.

Then Cephas and Lazarus went back to Bet Anya to tell the other disciples and Jesus' mother. But Miryam, still overcome with grief and now bewilderment, remained outside the tomb with two of her fellow female disciples, crying. As she wept, she bent over to look into the tomb and saw two angels in white, seated where Jesus' body had been, one at the head and the other at the foot. They asked her, "Woman, why are you crying?"

Distraught with grief and fear, she replied, "They have taken my Master away, and we don't know where they have put him."

Then the two angels, in clothes that gleamed like lightning, stood before Miryam and her companions. In their fright, the women bowed down with their faces to the ground, but the angels said to them, "Why do you look for the living among the dead? He is not here; he has risen! Remember how he told you, while he was still with you in Galilee: 'The Son of Man must be delivered into the hands of sinful men, be crucified, and on the third day be raised again.'" Then they bowed their heads, remembering the words. But when they looked up, the angels had disappeared.

At this, Miryam turned around and saw Jesus standing there, but she did not recognize him. "Woman," he said, "why are you crying? Who is it you are looking for?"

Thinking that he was the gardener, she said, "Sir, if you have carried him away, tell me where you have put his body, and I will get him."

Jesus looked at her with great affection and simply said, "Miryam."

Instantly recognizing his voice, Miryam turned toward him and cried out in Aramaic, "*Rabboni*!"—which means "teacher." She ran to Jesus, fell on her knees, and grasped his cloak.

"Do not hold on to me, for I have not yet returned to the Father," he said. "Go instead to my brothers and tell them, 'I am returning to my Father and your Father, to my G-d and your G-d.'"

So it was Miryam—the first of Jesus' female disciples—who was now the first to proclaim the good news about the risen Christ. Commissioned by Jesus himself, she, with the other women, ran to the male disciples with the news. She told them, "I have seen the Master!" And she went on to tell them everything that Jesus had said to her. But the male disciples did not believe her testimony or that of the other women, and, indeed, one of them even suggested that it was "merely a woman's fantasy" or delirium from grief. So the women went to tell some of the other Judaean disciples, hoping that they would listen.

Later that same day, two of the Judaean disciples were headed to a home in Emmaus, a village about seven miles from Yerushalayim. They were talking with each other about everything that had happened. While they were discussing these things, Jesus himself arrived and joined them on their journey. But they were prevented from recognizing him.

He said to them, "What are you talking about as you walk along?" They stopped, their faces downcast.

One, named Cleopas, replied, "Are you the only visitor to Yerushalayim who is unaware of the things that have taken place there over the last few days?"

"What things?"

"The things about Jesus of Netzerit. Because of his powerful deeds and words, he was recognized by G-d and all the people as a prophet. But our chief priests and our leaders handed him over to be sentenced to death, and they crucified him. We had hoped he was the one who would redeem Israel. All these things happened three days ago. But there's more: some women from our group have left us stunned. They went to the tomb early this morning and didn't find his body. They came to us saying that they had even seen a vision of angels, who told them he is alive. Some of those who were with us went to the tomb and found things just as the women said. But him, they did not see."

"How foolish you are, and slow of heart to believe all that the prophets talked about! Wasn't it necessary for the Messiah to suffer these things and then enter into his glory?" Then he interpreted for them the things written about himself in all the Scriptures, starting with Moses and going through all the prophets.

When they came to Emmaus, Jesus acted as if he was going on ahead. But they urged him, saying, "Stay with us. It's nearly evening, and the day is almost over." So he went inside to stay with them. After they had all taken their seats at the table, Jesus took the bread, blessed and broke it, and gave it to them. Their eyes were opened and they recognized him, but he disappeared from their sight. They said to each other, "Weren't our hearts on fire when he spoke to us along the road and when he explained the Scriptures for us?"

The men then raced back to Yerushalayim. They found the eleven remaining original disciples and their companions gathered together, saying to each other, "The Lord really has risen! He appeared to Cephas!" Then the two Judaean disciples described what had happened along the road and how Jesus was made known to them as he broke the bread.

That evening the disciples were together at Lazarus' home, with the doors locked for fear of the Jewish authorities, since they all knew where Lazarus lived. Jesus appeared and stood among them. He said, "Peace be with you!" After he said this, he showed them the wounds in his hands and side. The disciples were ecstatic at seeing the Lord, and most of them broke down and wept for joy.

Jesus said once more, "Peace be with you! As the Father has sent me, I am sending you." And with that, he breathed on them, saying, "Receive the Holy Spirit. If you forgive anyone his sins, they are forgiven; if you do not forgive them, they are not forgiven." With these words, Jesus disappeared as quickly as he had appeared, leaving the disciples once more in shock at what had just happened.

Thomas was not with the disciples when Jesus came. So when the others told him, "We have seen the Master!" he said to them, "Unless I see the nail marks in his hands and put my finger where the nails were, and put my hand into his side, I will not believe it." Several days went by and Jesus had not appeared again, so Thomas became even more skeptical and lacking in faith.

A week later, the disciples were in Lazarus' house again, and this time Thomas was with them. Though the doors were locked, Jesus came and stood among them and said, "Peace be with you!" Then he said to Thomas, "Put your finger here; see my hands. Reach out your hand and put it into my side. Don't be unbelieving: believe." Thomas fell down before Jesus and said to him, with tears streaming down his face, "My Master and my G-d!"

"Because you have seen me, you have believed," Jesus said. "Blessed are those who have not seen, and yet have believed." Then, once again, he disappeared from their midst.

After several more days had gone by, Cephas remembered that Jesus had said before his death that he would go before them into Galilee and meet them there. "Let's head north to Galilee," Cephas said, "and spend a little time fishing, reflecting on all that has happened. Our Master said he would meet us there, and I trust he will."

This sounded like a good plan to the others, not least because the authorities must have discovered by then that Jesus' body was missing from the tomb, and surely they would be searching high and low for the disciples. Lazarus said, "I'm coming with you. I would like to see the Galilee." Jesus' mother, however, had decided she would stay in Yerushalayim for some time with her family and friends, so she did not return to Galilee with them.

38

Recommissioning

THE ROADS WERE full of pilgrims returning to Galilee by the great north-south road, and the Galilean disciples were glad to be going home, away from the tense environment of Yerushalayim. They spent the first night in Kefer Nahum, and long before dawn, several of the disciples found themselves awake and seeking company.

"I'm going fishing," Cephas announced. Thomas, Nathan'el, and the sons of Zebedee went with him, as well as Lazarus and one of the other Judaean disciples. They left in the boat, but throughout that day and night, they caught nothing.

Early the next morning, Jesus stood on the shore, but the disciples did not realize that it was him. He called out to them, "Lads, haven't you caught any fish?"

"No," they answered with a grunt.

"Throw your net over the right side of the boat, and you will find some."

When they did this, they were unable to haul the net in because of the large number of fish. Then Lazarus, the disciple whom Jesus loved, said to Cephas, "It is the Master!"—because he remembered the story about the first time Jesus had gotten into a boat with Cephas, and what had happened then.

As soon as Cephas heard Lazarus say this, he threw his outer garment back on, for he had taken it off to fish, and jumped into the water to swim the hundred yards back to shore. The other disciples followed in the boat, towing the net full of fish. When they landed, they saw a fire of burning coals with fish cooking, and some bread. Cephas suddenly thought of the fire he had warmed his hands on in the courtyard of Caiaphas, a memory he did not cherish.

Jesus said to them, "Bring some of the fish you have just caught." Cephas climbed aboard the boat and dragged the net ashore. It was full of large fish, 153 to be exact; but even with so many, the net was not torn.

Jesus said to them, "Come and have breakfast." He took the bread and gave it to them, and did the same with the fish. This was the third time Jesus had appeared to his male disciples as a group, after being raised from the dead.

He said to all the disciples gathered on that morning, "I am sending you out now to spread the good news about me. And so you must go, baptizing people in G-d's name and making disciples, bearing in mind that I will be with you all along through the presence of G-d's Spirit, whom I will send to you when I return to the Father."

When they had finished eating, Jesus said to Cephas, "Simon son of John, do you love me more than these?"

"Yes, Master, you know that I love you."

"Then feed my lambs."

Again, using the fisherman's birth name, for Jesus was starting over with Cephas, he asked, "Simon son of John, do you truly love me?"

"Yes, Lord, you know that I love you."

"Then take care of my sheep."

Then Jesus asked a third time, "Simon son of John, do you love me?"

Cephas was hurt because Jesus had asked him a third time. He began to weep, and as the tears rolled down his face, he whispered in a voice filled with remorse, "Master, you know all things; you know that I love you."

"Then feed my sheep. Amen, amen, I say to you, when you were younger, you dressed yourself and went where you wanted; but when you are old, you will stretch out your hands, and someone else will dress you and lead you where you do not want to go." Jesus said this to indicate the kind of death by which Cephas would glorify G-d. Then he repeated the words that had started the long journey Cephas had taken: "Follow me!"

Cephas turned and saw that the disciple whom Jesus loved was following them. When Cephas saw Lazarus, he asked, "Master, what about him?"

Jesus followed Cephas' gaze, and said, "If I want him to remain alive until I return, what is that to you? You must follow me." Because of this, the rumor spread among the brothers that Lazarus would not die—not least because Jesus had already raised him from death once. But Jesus did not say that he would not die; he only said, "If I want him to remain alive until I return, what is that to you?"

Jesus did many other things as well. If every one of them were written down, even the whole world would not have room for the scrolls that would be written. But these things have been written so that you might begin to believe that Jesus, the divine and human Son of Man, was also the Son of the living G-d, the Messiah of the Jews, and the Savior of the world.

Afterword

You, Lord, are both lamb and shepherd. You, Lord, are both prince and slave.

You, peacemaker and sword-bringer, of the way you took and gave.

You, the everlasting instant; you, whom we both scorn and crave.

Clothed in light upon the mountain, stripped of might upon the cross,

Shining in eternal glory, beggar'd by a soldier's toss,

You, the everlasting instant; you, who are both gift and cost.

You, who walk each day beside us, sit in power at G-d's side.

You, who preach a way that's narrow, have a love that reaches wide.

You, the everlasting instant; you, who are our pilgrim guide.

Worthy is our earthly Jesus! Worthy is our cosmic Christ!

Worthy your defeat and vict'ry. Worthy still your peace and strife.

You, the everlasting instant; you, who are our death and life.

Alleluia!

—Sylvia Dunstan